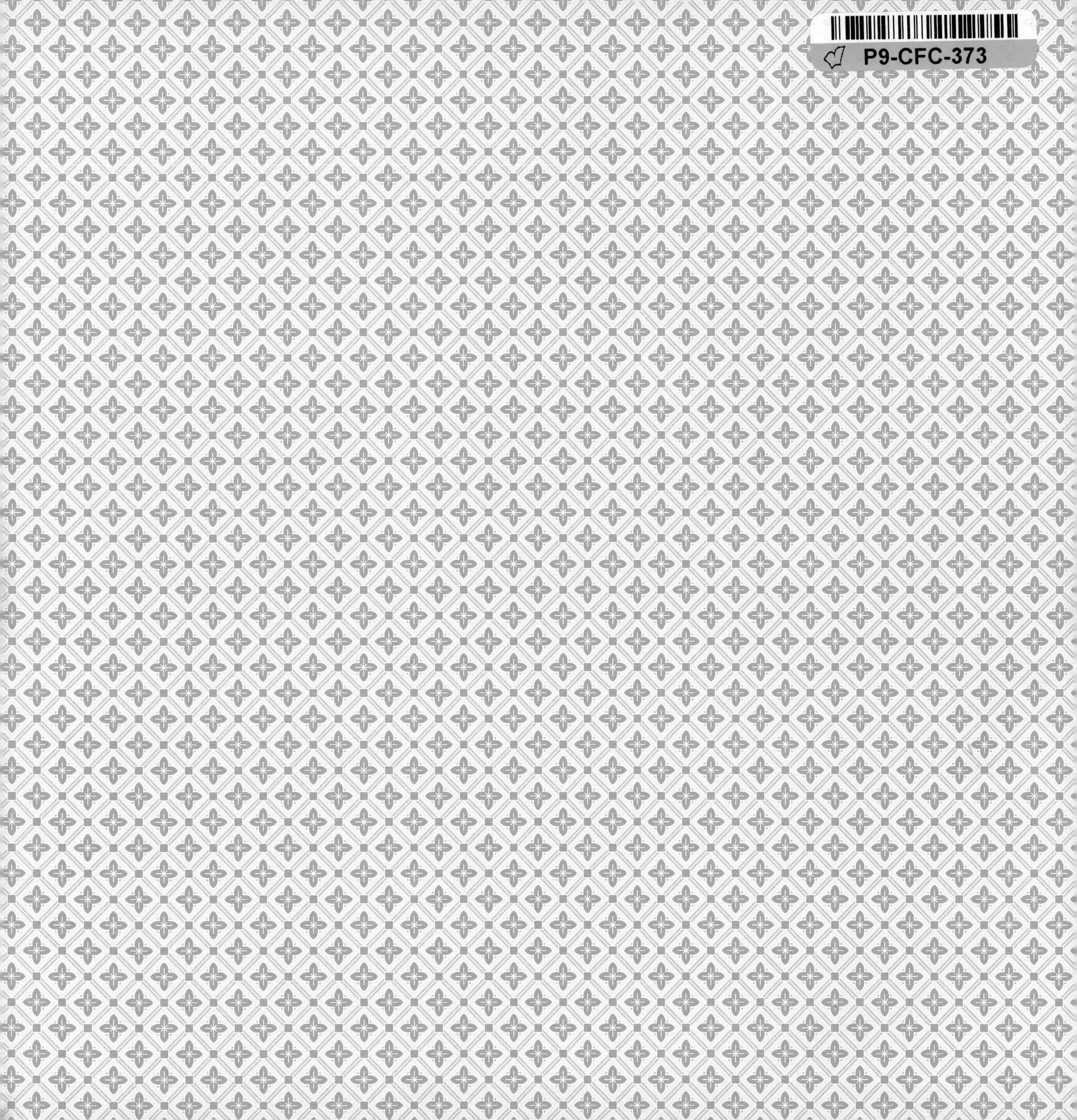
P9-CFC-373

The Ultimate Kitchen

Mary Wynn Ryan

Consultant:
Allison Murray Morris

Photo Editor:
Barbara H. Jacksier

Publications International, Ltd.

Mary Wynn Ryan has written about home furnishings and interior design for numerous publications, including *Woman's Day Decorating Ideas* magazine. She has served as Midwest editor of *Design Times* magazine and was director of consumer and trade marketing for the Chicago Merchandise Mart's residential design center, which included kitchen and bath products. She is president of Winning Ways Marketing, an editorial and marketing consulting firm that specializes in home design and decorating.

Allison Murray Morris (consultant) is the former editor of *Woman's Day Kitchen & Baths* and a frequent contributor to such magazines as *Kitchen & Bath Business, American Home Style and Gardening, Custom Builder, Woman's Day Home Remodeling,* and *Great American Kitchens.* She is the author of two books, *Kitchen Styles* and *Bathroom Styles.*

Barbara H. Jacksier (photo editor) is an editor, consultant, and frequent guest lecturer on home design topics. She is the editor of several decorating magazines for Harris Publications, including *Country Decorating* magazine's *Country Kitchens, Bedrooms & Baths* and *Country Collectibles.*

Illustrations (kitchen floor shapes): Donna M. Martin

All effort has been made to feature current products on the market. However, some products may not be available from a manufacturer or retailer after the publication date. Therefore, the product information depicted in this publication is presented only as a representation of the types of products available from a given commercial or manufacturing source.

Louis Weber, CEO
Publications International, Ltd.
7373 North Cicero Avenue
Lincolnwood, Illinois 60712

Manufactured in China.

8 7 6 5 4 3 2 1

ISBN: 0-7853-3374-6

Library of Congress Catalog Card Number: 00-101698

Contents

Whether your personal style leans toward country or cutting edge or somewhere in between, you can have the kitchen of your dreams.

Planning Your Dream Kitchen

A NEW KITCHEN is one of the most rewarding gifts you can give yourself and your family. The heart of your home, your kitchen is where late-night talks, homework sessions, and casual celebrations (the best kind!) happen naturally. It's where memories are made. Your kitchen is where you nurture your loved ones' souls as well as their bodies. So you want it to be as efficient, comfortable, and just plain beautiful as possible! But where do you start? The ideas and suggestions in this book will help you make that perfect new kitchen happen.

What Matters Most to You?

Elegant yet casual, this French country kitchen utilizes angled walls and a kitchen island/table that's also set on an interesting angle for a dramatic look. A pale marble floor and handsome wood cabinets add to the room's cozy appeal. ***Cabinets: Wood-Mode.***

THIS BOOK SHOWCASES hundreds of different kitchens, giving you beautiful, workable ideas to try. But another reason it includes so many different looks is to remind you that "the ultimate kitchen" means something different to everyone. Your dream kitchen may not suit your best friend, your sister, or the family down the street. So, enjoy your family's advice and your friends' interest in your project. But, for guidance, look to professionals who'll ask you a lot of questions prior to giving you a lot of advice.

Before you hire those pros, do some careful thinking about your dream kitchen. What do you like about your current kitchen? What do you dislike? Browse through this book, and tag pages showing kitchen designs and products you like. Buy a few pocket folders, and start saving photos, product catalogs, and clippings that can help your hired professionals understand your taste and needs. Check out Web sites that offer kitchen and design products, and if there's a kitchen design center near you, spend time window-shopping. You want to get an idea of what's available and what it costs. If you arm yourself with this information ahead of time, you'll have a better relationship with your professionals and a better chance of getting just what you want.

How can you get the kitchen that really fits and pleases you? Try these suggestions for starters:

- **Be a savvy spender.** Your first wish should be a kitchen that doesn't break the bank. Yesterday's conspicuous-consumption "status kitchen" is out, and today's deftly designed, personal-style kitchen is in. So start by asking for the most kitchen you can afford on your predetermined budget.
- **Nail the essentials down first.** If you have to choose, you're better off spending your money on top-grade design services rather than on upgraded materials. If you invest up front in a design that

gets the floor plan and essential elements right, you can always upgrade to luxury surfacing materials later. For example, make sure the kitchen island with outlets is in the right place now. You can change that laminate countertop to granite later, as you can afford it. It is a much costlier challenge to relocate the island and change the wiring later than it is to merely resurface. At the same time, you should buy the best products your budget can afford, especially if you have no plans for moving in the next five years.

- **Look at how you really live.** The best kitchen is a functional kitchen. Make sure yours fits how you really live. If you and your partner love to cook and entertain, don't settle for one oven, one sink, and no place to sit. If "Martha Stewart doesn't live here" is your motto, don't bother with two ovens and a six-burner restaurant stove. If your kids are at the do-it-yourself age, go for a roomy, top-of-the-line microwave installed near the fridge. If you come home from work late but still like to cook seriously, you may want to have a microwave installed near the stove for quick defrosting before cooking.

You get the idea. Your architect, kitchen designer, or other professional should ask you tons of questions about how you live as well as what you like. They'll walk you through your everyday life as it affects your kitchen. Your job is to answer candidly; their job is to translate your lifestyle needs into product and design solutions.

With courage and clever planning, your kitchen can be as individualistic as you are. This kitchen fits a homeowner who loves modern style, books, and lots of natural light—and it shows.

Just a few of the questions you'll be asked should include:

—How many people live in your household? What are their ages, and do any of them have special physical needs, including allergies?

—Do you have any special interests that need to be accommodated in the kitchen area, such as serious wine storage, laundry, window gardening, etc.? Do you need to watch small children while cooking, or do you want to make room for two cooks at a time?

—What is your budget? What's on your must-have list, and what's on your nice-to-have list?

Have fun thinking things through as best you can, and be sure to involve the rest of your family. It may be your five-year-old who remembers you've always wanted a pet port in the back door for the family cat, or your teen who lobbies for an adjacent mudroom/laundry room.

Love the Triangle

Fifty years ago, efficiency experts tracked the average housewife's steps in the kitchen and discovered that a natural pathway exists between the refrigerator, stove, and sink. The path between these three appliances is called "the work triangle," and the distance between them, along with how easy it is—or isn't—to reach them, is still the measure of kitchen efficiency.

The sides of your work triangle don't have to be equal, but the number of feet between range and sink, sink and fridge, and fridge and range should add up to something between 12 and 23 feet. (For example, range and fridge could be 3 feet apart, sink and fridge could be 8 feet apart, and range and sink could be 10 feet apart for a total of 21 feet.) For maximum efficiency and safety, make sure your design includes counterspace next to the open side of the fridge (either side, if your model is a side-by-side) for landing bags of groceries, as well as plenty of heat- and wet-resistant counterspace on both sides of the stove and sink for emergency landing of heavy, hot, or slippery cookware.

Today's additional appliances—a second dishwasher, a separate cooktop, etc.—may create extra work stations, which means additional triangles in your kitchen. In these cases, use extra care to make sure triangles don't create collision courses. For energy-saving reasons, it's best to separate the fridge and the range or oven if space permits. And if you've got an island, you'll need at least 4 feet between it and the nearest counter or appliance. Obviously, this all requires good planning and orchestration!

Shape Up

Big or small, basic or elaborate, most efficient kitchen designs fall into one of a few basic arrangements. Your existing kitchen probably fits one of these; a newly built house is likely to uti-

Warm wood teamed with cool marble and stainless steel give this chic L-shape kitchen its timeless flair. ***Designer: Maloos S. Anvarian, ASID, CCIDC, Design With Maloos. Dishwasher: Miele; stove and range hood: Thermador.***

lize one of them. Think about which appeals most to you.

- L-shape kitchens have one long "leg" housing two of the three basic appliances (range, fridge, sink) and one short "leg" housing the other. This layout often places the fridge at one end, the range at the other, and the sink in between. In a two-cook version, you might find two triangles: a sink and cooking surface at one end, and another sink and cooking surface at the other, with shared access to the fridge.
- U-shape kitchens have two "legs" of equal length, so the range and fridge are opposite each other and the three appliances are equal distance apart. A two-cook version might have a cooktop at each end with shared access to an island sink and the fridge on the wall opposite the sink.
- G-shape kitchens are L- or U-shaped with an added peninsula partly separating the work area from an adjoining breakfast area or family room. A two-cook version might have an extended peninsula and two cooking areas—one for an oven and one for a cooktop, both with access to a shared fridge and sink.
- Corridor or galley-shape kitchens, sometimes called step-saver kitchens, have range and sink on one wall, a fridge directly opposite, and a narrow (but not less than 36- to 40-inch) walkway in between. A two-cook version might feature an extra sink on the wall with the fridge, for two distinct triangles. Useful for very small spaces, this shape is most at risk for disruption if a main traffic lane is through the work area.

This G-shape kitchen uses knotty pine cabinetry and granite countertops to transition gracefully into a traditionally furnished dining area. **Designer: Douglas B. Leake, CKD, Custom Kitchens, Inc. Cabinets: Heritage Custom Kitchens.**

A dramatic U-shape kitchen with a tiered center island features flexible prep areas and good traffic flow. Two sinks and two 24-inch-wide refrigerators create separate work spaces for multiple cooks—an ideal setup for entertaining. **Designer: Lynn Monson, ASID, CKD, CBD, CID, Monson Interior Design, Inc.**

Plan for Your Whole Future

Do you have young children or grandchildren? want to stay in your home as long as possible as you age? have any kind of physical limitation?

"Universal design" is something you definitely want to consider. It goes way beyond designing walkways to accommodate wheelchairs.

Light and bright, this airy kitchen is a great example of universal-access design. Wheelchair-accessible base cabinet drawers and a roomy island allow for sit-down food prep. **Designer: Victoria Reginato, CKD, Premier Kitchens. Cabinets: *Ultra Craft.***

Universal design creates a versatile space that works well for every family member at every stage of life. Solutions as simple as bordering a countertop in contrasting-color tiles to mark the edge, increasing aisle width from 36 to 40 inches, or specifying no-scald faucets and wing-style faucet handles that don't require wrist-twisting can make a difference in your kitchen's long-term usefulness. If a family member has allergies or if you want to be particularly rigorous about ecological issues, you can even specify products made with special glues, colorants, and materials to meet those needs. And today's universal-design products are as attractive as their conventional counterparts, too. Ask your kitchen professional about them before you get started.

Style It Your Way

Do you love your home's architecture? Do you dote on the decorating style you've already established for the rest of your house? Now's the time to bring your kitchen's style in sync with it. A knowledgeable designer or architect can steer you toward products that meet today's needs while evoking the inspiration of the past. If your home is circa-1865 Victorian or 1930s art deco, you can have the fixtures, fittings, and furniture-style cabinets that create a great vintage look.

If you're building a new home from scratch, it may be time for a real break from your past. Take this opportunity to freely choose the style that warms your heart; one that makes you happy to get up in the morning and stagger out to make that first pot of coffee.

Kitchen appliances can't help but be contemporary, so they'll introduce a modern element to the most traditional setting. On the other hand, natural (or faux) stone and wood cabinets, countertops, and floors impart a timeless warmth to even the most up-to-date space. So it shouldn't be hard to go with the flow and introduce at least some elements of your other rooms' style into your kitchen. Flow is most easily achieved by mirroring a color or two, echoing architectural details, and repeating decorating motifs. After all the initial "oohs" and "aahhs" you expect to hear from first-time visitors, you'll want your new kitchen to fit in smoothly, as if it has always been a part of the house. This book includes a wealth of wonderful kitchen designs that will show you how to put it all together.

KITCHEN DESIGN and construction fall under four major categories. In your pursuit of the ultimate kitchen, you're sure to find the one that works for you.

New Construction

"New construction" refers to work done on a house that's being entirely built from the ground up. Normally, the decision to build a new home rests on more than just the need for a new kitchen. But the decision to build from scratch often provides the most leeway for creating the kitchen configuration you want. If, for example, you'd love the formal dining room, kitchen/breakfast room, and family room to all flow into one another, with the kitchen as the hub, new construction can make that happen for you with the stroke of a pen. If you want the washer and dryer right off the kitchen, you can have it—and a mudroom, too! If you want to watch the sunrise from your breakfast room and the sunset from your dining room, your wish is the architect's command.

Of course, the overall house and lot size will affect your kitchen's size, and your kitchen budget is just one part of your entire home-building budget. But in new construction, you can trade off square feet and dollars between the kitchen and other rooms for maximum flexibility.

Remodeling

Remodeling involves major changes that may take your kitchen in a whole new direction. Remodeling is what you're up to if you need to change the whole "footprint" of your kitchen to add space or reshape the room for better views or better access. While your existing home's size and site will affect how radically you can change your kitchen, you can make surprisingly big changes. Remodeling doesn't depend on what your old kitchen looked like, only on what your needs and wishes

Remodeling opened a cramped kitchen to tropical views while pairing fresh white with jungle greens in granite, ceramic tile, and wood stain. **Designers: Roxanne and David Okazaki, CKDs, The Cabinetree Design Studio. Cabinets: Heritage Custom Kitchens; refrigerator: Sub-Zero; range: Viking; range hood: Vent-A-Hood.**

Rope detailing enriches a classic renovation that opened this small kitchen to an adjacent family room. Crown moldings and hardwood flooring pull it all together. **Designer: Marilyn Woods, CKD, Marilyn Woods Design Associates. Tile countertop: Fireclay Tile.**

Where do you put a new kitchen in a 200-year-old house with a conservatory? In a new adjoining conservatory, of course. This add-on injects modern commercial pizzazz into classic calm. **Designer: Mary Kurtz, CKD, Mary Kurtz Kitchens.**

are and what your budget dictates. New built-in appliances and cabinetry, new windows and skylights, a new eat-in area or home office niche, a family room/kitchen combination, and more—anything's possible with remodeling.

Renovation

Renovation involves significant changes but is faithful to the spirit and overall look of your existing house. Renovating means making improvements with very few, if any, structural changes. If your home is historically significant, you may need—or even be required—to handle any upgrades with great respect for the existing style and structure. Since kitchens have changed much more radically over the past century than, say, dining rooms, the challenge of renovation is to preserve the best of the past while giving you a workable kitchen for today's lifestyle. Luckily, pre-WWII-vintage kitchens tended to be large, with an eat-in area and adjacent pantries. So creating a good-size kitchen in the existing space may prove easier than you think.

Decorative Changes

Decorative changes, or a kitchen face-lift, involve sprucing up without tearing down. This is cheaper and easier than remodeling or renovation but won't address major problems, such as lack of light, space, and connection to other rooms. If your kitchen basically suits you as it is, but you'd like a bit more efficiency or a fresher, more stylish appearance, decorative changes may be what you need. At its most ambitious, a facelift may include replacing some appliances, countertops, and flooring with high-performance, stylish upgrades. Or it may include simply changing the wallcoverings and window treatments and adding fresh accessories. A new look can make a well-planned kitchen more enjoyable to work and live in.

Whatever you choose, be sure your expectations are in line with what's possible, given the scope of the work and your budget. Veteran homeowners who've been through any of these productions agree: Even the ultimate kitchen is only a small part of your life, so keep things in perspective.

Of course you're eager to get started. But heed some advice from the experts and from people who've done the job already: Take your time at the beginning to make sure each decision reflects your taste and meets your needs. You'll want to live with and love this kitchen for a long time!

Your budget will have a lot to say about materials used in your new kitchen, but so will common sense. You don't want your kitchen to be a financial burden, so make sure you really need the high-end solution in each case.

Another way to stay in the black without closing off options too soon: Make a list of everything you'd love to have in your new kitchen. Now, divide this list into A) things you need and B) things you want but could live without for now. This will save time later and ensure you don't lop off something essential when you fall in love with a "could-live-without" item in the showrooms.

Most costs fall under the broad heading of Time (actual person-hours, or labor) or Materials. You can save money on both.

You can save a lot of money on labor if you buy basic cabinets, like these roomy wall models, and install them yourself. Movable pieces like this butcher-block–topped utility cart also stretch the budget. To create the look of a more luxurious kitchen, choose an elegant wallcovering and save again by hanging it yourself. ***Wallcovering: York Wallcoverings.***

Save Money on Labor

In construction, time is expressed as hourly rates paid to various workers on your project. One way to save big is to invest your time instead of theirs. Put in sweat equity wherever you're competent to do so. If you can steam off wallpaper, remove old moldings, and carry away debris yourself, you won't have to pay someone else to do it.

What kinds of labor can you perform yourself? Use common sense. Be careful about tearing out walls on your own (make sure you know where wiring, pipes, and such are located). And steer clear of removing old insulation that may contain asbestos or old paint that almost certainly contains lead. If your home has historical significance, get guidance from an expert before tackling anything.

When it's time to put on the finishing touches, you can paint the walls, screw on switchplates, and yes, pick up the debris rather than paying someone else to do it. The money you save on labor can pay for some of those luxurious material upgrades you crave!

Save Money on Materials

Marble and granite countertops; state-of-the-art imported fixtures and appliances; hand-crafted, hand-painted wall and floor tiles; custom cabinetry in high-end, furniture-grade woods . . . the list of luxury materials is endless. If you can't afford them all, choose the ones that matter most to you—and find artful substitutes for the rest. A few examples:

- **Marble and granite countertops.** If you make pastry, you'll want a marble inset in your countertop, but you don't need to be rolling in dough to have it. Compare the cost of real marble and granite to look-alike laminates, and you may decide on the synthetic for the rest of your countertops. Specify a rolled edge to eliminate the back wall seam. If you must have the real thing, specify marble or granite tiles: Nine-inch or 12-inch squares are easier to fabricate and install than running-foot slabs and, therefore, are much less costly. If famous-name solid-surfacing material is way out of your price range, look for similar solid-surfacing brands that are less expensive. Or choose a plain, matte-finish ivory laminate, and use a rolled edge.

Durable, dependable marble, with all its elegance, puts the island center stage. To save money, less costly surfacing is used on perimeter counters. ***Designer: Lois Perry Kirk, Kitchens Unique, Inc., by Lois. Cabinets: Heritage Custom Kitchens.***

- **Handmade, custom-colored, imported ceramic wall tiles.** Beautiful, artistic, and costly, hand-colored tiles may be too expensive to use throughout but just right as borders and accents. Choose a compatible plain tile for most of the installation, and save the custom pieces for eye-level areas such as the backsplash or a border around a breakfast nook window.
- **Luxury flooring.** Ceramic tile, oak planking with contrasting wood insets and butterfly ties, and marble or granite flooring may be out of reach, but today's handsome vinyl flooring isn't. All these looks and more are available at several price points. You probably know how easy no-wax vinyl is to keep looking new, but you may be surprised by how close to the natural materials these floors look. Choose sheet vinyl for seamless easy care, or, if your pattern includes smaller faux-tile designs, you may opt for tile squares you can install yourself. If you want the look of wood flooring, parquet is less costly than planking. The most practical alternative at a price? Wood-look laminates that get their realistic appearance from a photographic process that captures the graining and variations of genuine wood. For a cutting-edge look, consider concrete with color added during installation. It's an easy way to bring commercial kitchen chic home.
- **Custom cabinetry.** Many cabinets come in such a wide array of stock sizes and shapes, they assure a virtually custom fit. Use stock cabinets

Honoring charming Victorian style, this budget-savvy kitchen includes a stove backsplash made from leftover bath tiles. The homeowners also saved money by using a vintage drop-leaf table as a kitchen island instead of buying a new cabinetry unit. Wallcovering in rich, traditional colors gives the room a sense of luxury without a lot of expense. ***Wallcovering: York Wallcoverings.***

wherever you can, and have matching, custom pieces fabricated to fill in odd spaces. If your budget says pine or oak but your heart says cherry or maple, you may prefer painted rather than stained cabinets to disguise the more prominent grains of the lower-cost woods. The look of freestanding furniture in the kitchen is hot right now, so you may want to use mostly painted cabinets and splurge on a breakfront or other freestanding unit in the wood of your choice. To finish off the custom look, replace ho-hum hardware with novelty pulls and handles on cabinets and drawers. From pewter forks to verdigris brass leaves, a wealth of style-setting hardware options are available.

Investment Kitchen?

You want your new dream kitchen to meet your needs and reflect your tastes—right up until the day you want to put your house on the market. Then, you'll be glad if you kept an eye on what the average home-buyer in your price range is looking for. A consumer-pleasing kitchen is one of the top home-selling elements, but even an expensive, custom kitchen can detract if it's too individualistic.

Appropriate upgrades can return as much as 70 to 90 percent or more of their cost to you at resale time and make it much easier for you to get your price on the home. When making decisions about materials, keep these tips in mind:

- Upgrades to better-performing, basic appliances or windows, for example, almost always add to both the sales appeal and the value of your home.
- Don't over-improve beyond what's typical for new or improved kitchens in your home's price range. A $100,000 kitchen in a $150,000 house may not yield the financial gains you think it will at resale time.
- When it comes to flooring, countertops, and other installed products that are available in many fashion colors and patterns, think twice before making a strong fashion statement. You don't want to date your kitchen or turn off your best prospects.
- Keep it simple when it comes to sinks, faucets, and other fixtures and fittings. If you're tired of shiny stainless, a brushed pewter-look stainless is luxurious; a bright red-enameled stainless may turn some people off. A gooseneck faucet that lets you wash big pans is a great innovation; a novelty-style faucet, although easy enough to replace, may give buyers pause.
- Stick with neutrals for installed products, especially if they're not luxury-grade. Midtone neutrals show wear the least; light-colored neutrals give a spacious, bright feeling. Be a bit careful with black unless the kitchen is huge and gets lots of natural light.
- Crave an adventurous scheme? Express yourself with wallcoverings (paint plus borders are easiest to change), seat cushions, window treatments, and accessories.

THE MOST IMPORTANT step in a successful kitchen project is selecting the right people to work on the job. Because much kitchen work is structural, it's essential—for legal and insurance reasons—that the work be performed according to the building codes of your area. And to be sure all work is done appropriately, you'll want to hire professionals for every aspect of the job in which you are not personally an expert.

When a high-rise homeowner wanted the warmth of a Mission-style kitchen, the designer rose to the occasion with a natural mix of wood and marble. ***Designer: The Cabinetree Design Studio. Cabinets: Heritage Custom Kitchens.***

For any structural work, you'll need a licensed architect or design/construction firm. You'll also want to use licensed contractors and skilled tradespeople, and you may want the specific expertise and creativity of a certified kitchen designer (CKD) or an interior designer with a lot of kitchen design experience. Whomever you hire, you'll rely on their expertise to guide you through technical issues, and you'll count on their integrity in working within your budget. What's more, your experts and their crews will be in your home and around your family for the life of the project. So make sure they really deserve your trust!

Check the Basics

Check with the attorney general's office in your state and with your local Better Business Bureau to be sure there are no unresolved complaints against the professional you're considering. For contractors, ask to see property damage, liability, and workers' comp insurance. (Don't take their word for it; tell them your lawyer insists you see each individual policy. Note the policy number, dates the policy is in effect, and the name, address, and phone number of each company providing coverage. Before work starts, call to be sure policies are still in force.) If building permits are needed, make sure they're made out in the contractor's name, not yours. This way, the contractor, not you, is responsible for rectifying any building code violations.

For every professional, ask to see samples/photos of similar work performed for others, and request contact information so you can call those customers. Ask for a dozen references, not just two or three; you want to know the firm has a good track record. Then, call three or four of those references. Ask if their projects were completed on schedule, if the pro was responsive to their calls, and if he/she kept them informed about the progress of the project. If you'll be living in your home while the work is being done, ask if the workers left the place "broom clean" at night or in a mess; if they woke the baby with loud music or were easy to live with. Ask if they would hire him/her again or recommend him/her to family and friends.

When you meet with your prospective professionals, be sure you have an elementary rapport with them. Do you believe they're knowledgeable? Honest? Pleasant and responsive? Reliable and unflappable? Do they seem interested in your needs, your lifestyle, and your dreams? If anything "just doesn't feel right," keep looking. Chemistry counts!

Finally, make sure the pro gives you a quote fully describing the work, the specific products to be used (by brand name, type, model number, color, size, etc.), the costs, the starting and completion dates (plus conditions of, and penalties for, nonperformance), and the terms of payment. You won't need the same full-blown contract for a $1,500 job that you would for a job worth $30,000 or $150,000, but be sure the basics are covered in writing. Get detailed drawings of the project to ensure that you, the designer, and the contractor are envisioning the same kitchen. Every aspect of the project should be included—from the location and number of outlets to the size of doorways and windows. Changes down the road can be costly and frustrating. Keep in mind: It's your home and your money.

A hexagonal counter that follows the room's lines and an appealing array of French-inspired details indicate that a confident design sense was at work here. **Designer: Bruce Colucci, CKD, Le Gourmet Kitchen. Cabinets: Kountry Kraft.**

The Best of Bon Appetit
Bon Appetit

Picking out ingenious new appliances and beautiful new cabinets is great fun, but first you and your kitchen professional will need to figure out where those new treasures will be located. Unless your new kitchen is part of a brand-new house, you'll need to decide how much change to make in the "footprint" of your existing kitchen. For big savings, experts advise working within existing load-bearing walls and plumbing lines. And remember that whatever the shape of the kitchen itself, there's bound to be a configuration that gives you an efficient work triangle. You won't have to choose between great looks and great performance!

Making use of every light-catching opportunity, this galley kitchen's roomy, cushioned window seat offers an unusual but perfect spot from which to kibbitz with the chef or curl up with a good book.

Sizing up—and Shaping Up

WHETHER IT'S MINI, midsize, or massive, your kitchen can be designed to meet your needs and look beautiful, too.

SMALL, MEDIUM, OR LARGE

- **Small: Cozy and Carefully Engineered.** If your kitchen is tiny, try to steal some space from an adjoining pantry or closet, or even a few feet from the next room. If there's just no way to borrow extra square footage, see if you can visually open up the space: Add or enlarge a window, install a skylight, break through an interior wall into an adjacent dining or family room, or even break through the ceiling to create a cathedral that will dramatically create visual expansion. To maximize work space, consider an island on casters or a peninsula with hinged, drop-down sections. To make the most of storage space, run cabinets all the way up to the ceiling, and use pot racks and other overhead hooks that make use of ceiling space. Outfit drawers and cupboards with clever interior fittings—dividers, lazy Susans, and so on—to keep physical clutter at bay, and avoid visual clutter by using solid, pale colors that blend into one another. For an eat-in option, include a slender snack bar with overhanging counters that allow the stools to be tucked out of the way. And enjoy the advantages of small kitchens: They're naturally step-saving and cozily friendly.

An amusing border of 1940s-era cookie jars draws the eye upward in this kitchen, diverting attention away from its small size. Windowpane-check wallcovering, even on the island, creates subtle dimension. **Wallcovering: York.**

Fresh-picked vegetables cavort on contemporary wallcoverings and sprightly borders in this fun, retro-style kitchen. Open shelving and lots of white add to the airy, welcoming atmosphere, perpetuating the illusion of spaciousness in this small kitchen. **Wallcovering: York.**

Little wonders: This small kitchen uses classic, space-expanding white; an old-fashioned, cabriole-legged sink; a tiny table-as-island; and a New Orleans cuisine-inspired wallcovering border to set a chic scene. **Wallcovering: York.**

• **Midsize: Convenient and Comfortable.** Most homes have midsize kitchens, which, with a modest amount of intelligent improvement, can function like big ones. In both new and older homes, opening the kitchen to an adjoining family room creates a "great room" effect that gives the spacious feeling of an expanded kitchen. Other design tactics can make your midsize kitchen seem even bigger and better. Strive for maximum-length unbroken runs of work space; for example, locate the range at the end of a counter, not in the middle. By taking advantage of every clever, in-drawer storage solution recommended for small kitchens, you may be able to save enough space for a big-kitchen option like a second sink or a desk nook. If an island takes up too much space, consider a practical, tiered peninsula with work space on the kitchen side and a snack bar/serving counter on the family room side. Other dining options include a built-in dining nook with bench seating and a peninsula table, or a table with chairs on one side and a built-in banquette on the other. When decorating, keep colors light and patterns simple to maximize visual spaciousness, but if the kitchen opens into an adjoining room, repeat some elements in both rooms for continuity.

• **Large: Impressive and Entertaining.** More than ever, today's kitchens are rooms for living. Space for couple or communal cooking, doing homework, enjoying hobbies, watching TV, and more are all part of many people's wish lists, and that translates into bigger-than-ever rooms. Following that trend, today's new homes typically sport generously sized kitchens. In an older home, space for a big kitchen often comes from building an addition. More space allows homeowners to indulge in more work surfaces and more kinds of them (butcher block for cutting, marble for pastry-making, granite for everyday good looks, and so on). Large kitchens have ample space for amenities such as strategically placed islands; more than one wall oven and sink; a second dishwasher; and/or a full-size, side-by-side fridge plus state-of-the-art refrigeration drawers located within cabinets anywhere in the room. A comfortable snack bar or breakfast bar, an informal dining area, and a built-in desk or computer

A large kitchen can successfully handle the dramatic contrast of Beidermeier-style light maple with ebony piping around cabinet and appliance panels.
Designer: Greg Meyer, Kitchen Design Studio of New Canaan, Inc.

workstation are other options. A big kitchen also allows more latitude in decoration and design, including dark cabinets and wall colors, dramatic decorative effects, and sharply contrasting colors and patterns, so you can have it your way.

Solutions for Every Shape

Most rooms in the house are rectangular, but kitchens aren't most rooms. If your kitchen is square, has multiple angles, or even has irregular shapes, you're not alone. In kitchens, even though function comes first, with careful planning you won't have to sacrifice an attractive layout. New construction obviously offers the best chance for orchestrating the kitchen shape you prefer, but don't feel tied to the typical rectangle. A pentagon (a five-sided shape with the long side abutting the rest of the house and the points facing the garden) or a hexagon (a six-sided shape with a long wall available for a banquette or counter as well as a long wall abutting the rest of the house) are just two of the many intriguing options you may consider. While unusual shapes may seem most compatible in a very contemporary house, they also fit in nicely with other styles: Think of the hexagonal or even round turret rooms used since medieval times! Romantic, individualistic room shapes are enjoying a postmillennium renaissance among homeowners. What's especially fun is that you can specify round or hex-shaped sink bowls and other accoutrements that echo the shape of your room.

If changing the overall shape of your kitchen isn't an option, don't despair: With some savvy storage solutions, you can make use of just about any existing configuration. Plus, semi-custom and stock lines offer a slew of solutions and can certainly be arranged for a customlike fit, saving you some money. Many kitchen cabinet-makers offer custom options in the same woods and designs as their stock units, so you can use the more economical stock cabinets wherever they work well and fill in the problem areas with custom units. On the other hand, today's trend is toward a mix of cabinets of different heights and in several complementary finishes and colors for a freestanding, innovative look. If this concept appeals to you, why not take a tip from designer showrooms and play up those quirky corners and odd angles? They may be just the thing to give your kitchen its one-of-a-kind personality!

If your existing kitchen is not uniformly shaped but you yearn for a traditional look, you can use tried-and-true visual tactics to correct some irregularities. For example, a long, narrow "bowling alley"-shaped galley space will look more spacious if you: 1) fill one of the long walls with windows that visually widen the space and/or 2) paint the short walls with either a bright color or a dark, warm color that captures the eye.

Because cabinets and appliances do physically extend into the room, you can make them less visually obtrusive by minimizing the contrast between backsplash walls and cabinets. You can do this in one of two ways: 1) keep cabinets and walls similar in shade or tint, so they blend together, or 2) bring the backsplash forward visually with a colorful, attention-getting tile design. Also, keep in mind that dark cabinets and black glass-front appliances grab attention, while light ones recede, making the wall they're on seem farther away. Other expanders include windows; light sources; pale, solid colors; polished, reflective surfaces such as polished granite or ceramic tile; and large tiles, either plain or with simple patterns, laid on the diagonal. (This diagonal-tile trick works especially well on floors.)

A long, narrow island is key in this industrial-strength, T-shape kitchen design. A built-in commercial stove and refrigerator, steel cabinets, and Flash Gordon–inspired overhead lighting reinforce the bold, sleek statement.

To make your kitchen ceiling look higher, placing items of interest above the soffit level does the trick. The tops of cupboards are a great place to store little-used items or show off collectibles safely. If your kitchen has an unusually high ceiling, you can afford to visually lower it a bit by making it a vivid or dark color. On the other hand, if you want the ceiling to look higher than it is, let it soar by painting it a pale hue.

What Shape Is Your Work Triangle?

In kitchen geometry, the work triangle is the shape that connects the sink, cooktop, and refrigerator. The work triangle is the functional center of every kitchen.

Studies have shown that in the most efficient kitchens, the three legs of the work triangle add up to at least 12 feet but no more than 23 feet. Of course, your kitchen's basic shape and size will influence the type of work triangle that fits best. Regardless of the perimeter shape of the room, most kitchens are organized around one of several basic kitchen layouts, each with its own type of triangle. One's right for you!

- **U-Shape:** This shape puts the stove, fridge, and sink each on a different wall and offers a very compact triangle that lets you prepare a meal while walking the shortest distance. It works best with the sink (the most-used element) in the center of the "U" and the fridge at one end of a run

Near Right: *Ideal for kitchens with a square work space, the U-shape work triangle is compact and practical, with each of the three elements (range, refrigerator, and sink) located on a different wall.*

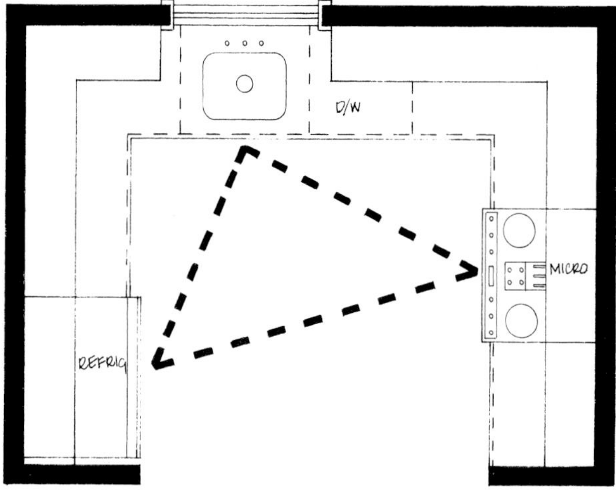

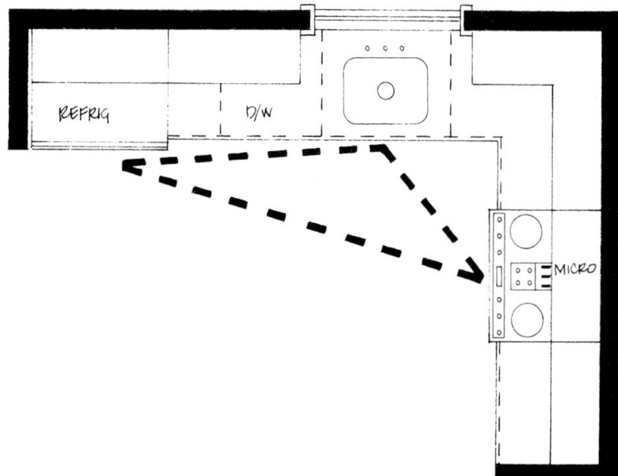

Below: *Breezy and modern, this U-shape kitchen is an efficient, compact design that saves steps and makes the most of an expansive window. Diagonally set, ceramic tile countertops enhance the clean look.*

of counters to avoid breaking up a work surface. This shape works well in a kitchen that's nearly square or in a kitchen where you want to tightly define one end of a larger space as the basic work area, with an island set in the open end of the "U," perhaps fronting onto the family room or breakfast room.

- **L-Shape:** This shape uses two walls of the kitchen for the three points of the work triangle. Often, the fridge is at one end of the long leg of the "L," the sink is toward the center of the same wall, and the stove is perpendicular, on the short leg of the "L." In contrast to the U-shape kitchen, the "L" has a long, rather than a short, wall facing into the rest of the room. Room traffic does not cross into the triangle, and, since this design uses only two walls, the triangle is long and relatively narrow, allowing for a more open layout. This setup is well-suited to a large room where the kitchen shares space with a family room. Additional counterspace may further lengthen one leg of the "L."

Above: *The L-shape kitchen's narrow, long layout allows for a large work area and lots of open space. The long leg of the triangle usually houses the fridge and sink; the stove is then located on the short leg.*

- **G-Shape:** This shape features one appliance on each of two walls and the third appliance on a peninsula that separates the work area from an

Custom-stenciled flooring around the granite-topped island and flower gardens "growing" on ceramic tile backsplashes add charm to this L-shape, Shaker-style kitchen. **Designer: Linda Daly, ASID, Olde Fields Farm.**

adjoining breakfast area or family room. If housing the cooktop in the accessible peninsula worries you (for safety reasons), you can always put the sink there instead and locate the cooktop on a full wall within the kitchen itself. Alternatively, put the cooktop on the peninsula, but create a safety margin by making the peninsula a tiered affair, with the cooktop at least six inches lower than the serving ledge.

Whatever your plan, the sink should take central position if at all possible, as it's used more often than either the refrigerator or the stove. If you locate the sink on the same wall as the stove, with the main work area in the middle, you won't drip water on the floor when you go from the sink to the cooktop. When placing the refrigerator, make sure the single-door model, when open, faces into the work triangle, not out of it.

Be sure you've allotted ample counterspace right next to any appliance: You'll want to set down heavy grocery bags near the fridge and slippery wet crystal next to the sink. It's especially important to have enough space (an absolute minimum width of 18 inches, and preferably 24 to 36 inches) right next to the cooktop, range, and oven, and on at least the opening side of the microwave and fridge. If you're using laminate countertops elsewhere in the kitchen, use heat-resistant material, such as ceramic tile, to create "landing space" near cooking appliances.

Peninsula dining on an angle leaves the kitchen triangle clear; diagonally set floor tiles anchor the subtly exciting scheme. **Designer: Joe McDermott & Diane Wandmaker, CKD, Kitchen Studio.**

Useful for very small spaces, corridor kitchens tend to have a range and sink on one wall, with a fridge directly opposite. Unfortunately, this setup puts the work triangle right in the middle of household traffic.

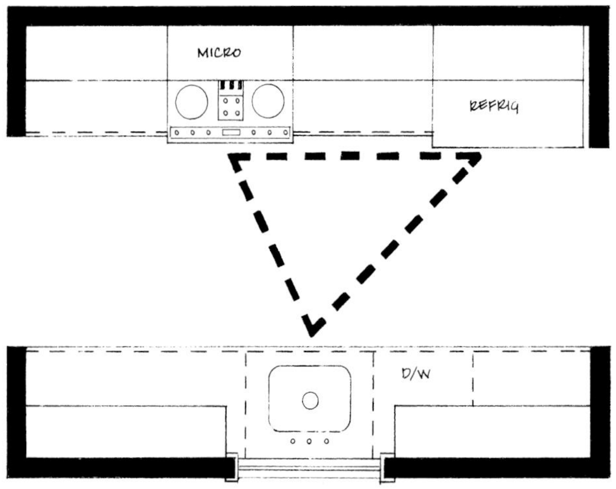

Great Little Galleys

Kitchens that work in small or narrow spaces deserve mention because they're able to fit the same essentials—stove, sink, fridge, work surfaces, and cabinets—into what are often pretty snug situations. Named for the food preparation areas of ships, galley kitchens come in a couple of styles.

This step-saving galley kitchen packs enormous charm in a small space. Curved wood countertops and lots of white expand the limited space, while the Wedgwood-inspired cabinet detailing and the ragged walls recall an elegant 18th-century townhouse.

- **Corridor.** This shape puts two points of the triangle on one wall and the third point on the opposite wall (most often the sink and the stove are placed on the same wall, with the fridge opposite). The length of the room will determine how much space there will be for cabinets and work surfaces. Corridor kitchens are often used where there is no other pathway to the next room and the traffic flows right through the work triangle. While this configuration is a step-saving solution, for safety as well as efficiency this setup should be avoided if at all possible, as should any design that allows household traffic to break into the triangle.
- **One-Wall.** This shape lines up the fridge, sink, and stove on one wall. It foregoes the step-saving convenience the triangle affords, as the user needs to walk farther from one end of the kitchen to the other, especially if there is to be adequate countertop space. A popular solution is to station one or more islands opposite the wall of appliances. If wiring can be added in the floor, the island can be stationed near the refrigerator and can hold the microwave and other small appliances. A tiered island allows for some simple types of food prep on the lower, kitchen side and a snack counter on the higher side, facing into the adjoining room. A one-wall kitchen is a practical choice for tiny spaces. It also can be tucked conveniently behind closed doors in a wall alcove, so it's great for second kitchens in recreation rooms, studios, or even master suites.

THE SIZE AND SHAPE of your kitchen will influence your work triangle layout, but your personal tastes and preferences will really come into play when it comes to choosing what special elements to include in your ultimate kitchen.

Cooking by Two or by Crew

More and more couples are cooking together just for the fun of it or to feed a horde of friends. In some cases, it's a matter of cooking with, not just for, a crowd, as guests help chop, wash, and prep as well as chat. For many families, cooking is also a favorite group activity, whether they enjoy a weekly homemade-pizza night every Sunday or an annual Christmas cookie bake-a-thon. A successful multi-cook kitchen includes multiples of at least one basic appliance (usually the sink or cooktop) that creates several separate workstations. These stations may share one or more of the other basics elements, or, if space allows, they may be entirely independent triangles.

The classic triangles have been updated for today's two-cook needs. In an L-shape kitchen-for-two, twin triangles may be created by adding an extra sink and an extra cooktop that share access to the refrigerator. A new U-for-two might feature two cooktops with shared access to an island sink and the fridge opposite, on the enclosed leg of the "U." The new G-shape kitchen might offer dual baking and surface cooking with one work area including a sink and cooktop and the other a sink and the oven, with both sharing access to the fridge.

In a shared kitchen, several people are working with hot, wet, and sharp items in one space. Safety basics include wide-enough traffic paths (at least 36 inches) to minimize collisions; nonslip flooring; and ample, heat-resistant landing spaces on both sides of every cooking appliance. Smart upgrades, especially when youngsters will be underfoot, are

For the family that cooks together, this kitchen features three granite-topped work stations, one with a cooktop and two with sinks. A tiered approach creates a perfect spot for casual dining and serving guests. ***Designer: Kitchens & Baths By Louise A. Gilmartin.***

rounded corners on cabinets and other kitchen furniture and well-designed knife racks or blocks to discourage chefs from leaving cutting tools on counters.

Let's Eat In

The formal, separate dining room has passed in and out of vogue over the decades, but the option of eating in the kitchen has always held appeal. The informal, efficient design of an eat-in kitchen is ideal for today's casual, fast-paced lifestyle. At the same time, today's tastes are distinctly more luxurious than they were a couple of decades ago. Fortunately, unless you yearn for an authentic period home, there's no reason why you can't have a kitchen dining setup that's both easygoing and opulent. Depending on the size of your kitchen, you have a number of choices for creating an eat-in kitchen. Today's savvy design solutions and coordinated products ensure that any option you choose will fit right in and look great.

Opulence comes to casual dining in this villa-style kitchen featuring a tumbled-marble counter with reeded columns, dramatic arches, and French 18th-century-style, counter-height chairs. ***Designer: Lila Levinson, ASID, CKD, CID, Accent On Design.***

- **Counter Dining.** Where space is slim or where the users have no special needs, a breakfast bar looks great. A breakfast bar's informality and slim silhouette lends itself naturally to a casual, contemporary scheme, but if your kitchen is opulently traditional, using the same materials for the counter and bar will tie it in perfectly. Imaginative counter stools can be great decorating assets. Make sure the counter overhang is deep enough to accommodate knees comfortably, and, if your stools don't have footrests, make sure your bar has a footrest ledge or rail.

  A two-tiered peninsula or island can house a sink or cooktop on the lower, kitchen side with room for two to four diners opposite. If the peninsula or island houses only a small sink, there's usually plenty of room to seat a number of diners on the same level as the work surface. (A cooktop requires more space and, if possible, the barrier of a different level for safety's sake.) Ideally, allow at least 42 inches from the

Fitting snugly into an arched nook, this built-in dining area with comfortable bench seats is a charming, cozy way to carry out the cottage kitchen look.

open end to the opposite wall, and don't locate the fridge or wall oven opposite, where an open door would block traffic. Allow at least 18 inches and preferably 24 inches of elbow room for each diner. And if breakfast never will be your thing, rest assured your cozy nook or chic bar will work just fine for after-school and midnight snacks.

- **Breakfast Nooks.** If you have a bit more available space or want a more traditional, cozy look, you might consider adding a breakfast area with built-in banquette seating. A bay window alcove, with a banquette serving as a window seat and with pull-up chairs on the other side of the table, is charming if you can manage it. You can create a welcoming air with plump bench or stool cushions that carry your color scheme.

No matter how small your kitchen or how rushed your schedule, there is almost always a way to work a little breakfast into the equation. The breakfast nook with fitted bench or banquette seating is a cozy solution that works well in ethnic or country/cottage kitchen design schemes. It's also a cute solution in retro settings inspired by a '50s malt shop booth. The table may be freestanding or may be a peninsula, with one end anchored to the wall or to a run of cabinets. The coziest breakfast nook setup features benches that are parallel, with the table between. For a more relaxed, open layout, the benches may be placed perpendicular to one another, with the table spanning the open side. A breakfast nook can be a comfortable solution where space is scant, because benches require much less floor space than chairs. If your family includes a mix of young and not-so-young, a breakfast nook may be a perfect—and practical—alternative. Benches are safer than counter stools for young children, and, because the table is a conventional height, it is accessible to wheelchair users.

High style meets high-rise: A row of multitiered cabinets looks like a sleek, architectural room divider from the living area but houses a microwave and storage space on the kitchen side. ***Designer: Roxanne Okazaki, CKD, The Cabinetree Design Studio.***

- **Eat-in Kitchens.** For large kitchens, or those that feature a natural alcove, dining tables that seat anywhere from four to 12 people are a good option. You can have fun picking out chairs that complement your own personal taste, from heirloom traditional to classic modern glass-and-metal. Another option you may consider is having an island or table made of the same material as your cabinets or countertops. In keeping with the informal nature of kitchen dining, consider small armchairs all around, not just at the head and foot of the table. A round table is a friendly choice and is safer for an active family or in a smaller space. In the dining area of your kitchen, away from the stove, you can define a welcoming space with more elaborate curtains or draperies than you would use at a window in the work area. For continuity's sake, match or coordinate your eating-area window treatments with those in the work area. Coordinate window treatments and tabletop textile colors with seating cushions for an inviting, total look.

Specialties of the House

Kitchens come in all shapes and sizes, which accounts for a lot of their challenge—and a lot of their appeal. The same cabinets, appliances, and surfacing materials can look entirely different in someone else's home than in yours. Stock cabinets can be given a unique look with virtually unlimited specialty finishes and a change of hardware. If your budget can accommodate custom cabinets, your choices are even greater. Countertop materials already come in a great array of choices, but they can be customized even further with special routing or inset bands of another color or material. The same goes for flooring, walls, and in-kitchen dining furniture. So even if your kitchen is small and ordinary, it's not hopeless! You can transform it into a remarkable space unlike anybody else's. Manufacturers and designers have seen it all, and the end result is that you can have all the amenities you want and need, even in a tiny kitchen. Savvy, space-saving products are available for the owner of the apartment-size condo, co-op, or townhouse kitchen. You'll find that convenience doesn't have to come only in the large economy size.

To create a distinctive space, your first move is to look at your kitchen with an eye to what might serve as a focal point. A large window, alcove, or long wall can be the start. Take advantage of a bank of beautiful windows with an eye-catching counter that runs the length of the window wall. If you love to entertain and are lucky enough to have ample space, consider setting your room up to include two back-to-back kitchens; one with a full-size range, a fridge, ovens, and a sink, and the other with an ice-maker, a wine chiller, a second sink, a mini-fridge, and a microwave, plus an abundance of storage. Pretty much anything you dream up can be executed with the help of a talented design team. It's up to you!

Whether your space is large or small, and whether the end result you want is pretty or pretty wild, you'll do best if you stick close to the following basic recommendations.

—Try to keep the straight-line distance between the sink, fridge, and cooktop between 12 and 23 feet.

—Position the sink between the other two appliances, since it's used most often. (The sink's location may depend on pre-existing plumbing lines.)

—Allow for 36 inches of counterspace to the right and 30 inches to the left of the range and sink if at all possible; if not, allow a minimum of 24 inches and 18 inches.

—It's tempting to place a tall fridge and built-in wall oven next to each other, but try not to; each needs its own landing space on both sides of the appliance for safety.

—Try to include a minimum of 10 linear feet of both base cabinets and upper cabinets.

—Utilize lazy Susans to make potentially wasted corners fully functional.

—Use pull-out drawers rather than reach-in, conventional cabinets for greatest convenience. If you're retro-fitting existing cabinets, have pull-out trays installed.

—Consider barrier-free design and products. They make life easier for children, pregnant women, and seniors as well as individuals with disabilities. They'll also add to the longevity of your kitchen.

Winding its way around an extraordinary kitchen, this serpentine-shaped run of cabinets includes two sinks, a drop-in cooktop, and more, all sleekly topped by regal granite counters. Handsome hunter-green base cabinets with simple brass pulls are classically elegant. **Designer: Lois Kirk, Kitchens Unique, Inc., by Lois.**

Special Settings

The Lure of the Islands

A kitchen island and its cousin, the peninsula, can vastly expand the design potential and convenience of just about any kitchen. Among the earliest islands were farm tables that gave cooks extra work surfaces and doubled as informal dining stations. Today, a homeowner has the option of islands made of the same materials as the base cabinets and countertop for an integral look. On the other hand, the latest trend is leaning back toward a freestanding look, with upper cabinets, base cabinets, and countertop materials in a mix of materials and colors. In this scenario, any freestanding piece of furniture with at least one part standing at about counter height can function as an island. Most homeowners prefer a piece that offers hidden cabinets, open shelves, or a combination of the two in addition to another work surface. In a more high-tech kitchen, lower storage may also include a host of refinements such as wine racks and refrigerated drawers.

In many kitchens, the island is used as an extra workstation, adding to the usefulness of the work triangle or corridor kitchen. In others, it's used as a low, casual divider defining the perimeter of the kitchen where it meets the family room or breakfast room. In either case, if you add in-floor wiring, plumbing, and gas lines, the possibilities for an island's usefulness are endless. Just about any appliance can be located in an island if the plumbing and electrical wiring are planned in. A wine rack, a gourmet wine chiller, an under-cabinet refrigerator, and an ice-maker on the family room side are very nice options. On the kitchen side, add a second dishwasher, a microwave, or even an under-cabinet wall oven. In a small or medium-size kitchen, one of the most popular uses of an island is as a place to house the sink. The option of facing toward the family room is so attractive that a kitchen island sink has replaced the classic under-the-window sink in many homes. In a larger kitchen, the island may house a second sink. When combined with

Rustically romantic, this medieval-inspired kitchen features handcrafted floor and backsplash tiles and a granite-topped island with lighted display shelving behind glass-front doors. **Designer: Kitchens Unique, Inc., by Lois.**

Opposite: *The dark and light contrast in this bistro-inspired kitchen makes the furniture-style island stand on its own. With ample counterspace to roll out pastry, a gooseneck faucet, and a table-style extension, it's a serious cook's dream workspace.*

This hip, modern kitchen takes the cake. Practicality coexists with design as the island houses a sink, a cooktop, wine storage, bookshelves, and a pop-up TV. **Designer: Janine Jordan, CKD, IIDA, IDS, JJ Interiors. Laminate: Wilsonart.**

easy access to the microwave and the fridge, this setup creates a secondary work triangle.

Your needs and tastes will help determine what kind of island you should have. In a smaller space, you'll get maximum storage, convenience, and a neat appearance if you specify cabinets on both sides of the kitchen island so that dishes can be stashed or removed from either side. For a stylish, freestanding-furniture look that's especially at home in traditional settings, specify an island with table legs and a low shelf for open display and storage. The common kitchen principle of extending every countertop at least an inch beyond the cabinets to prevent dribbling spills down cabinet fronts especially applies to islands. Obviously, you'll need significantly more overhang for knee room (at least 15 inches) if your island is used as a snack table or as a higher snack counter with stools (18 inches).

One of the most dramatic, popular island designs is two-tiered, with food prep on the kitchen side and counter seating on the other. A sink can be stationed either on the same level as the eating counter or on a waist-high work counter with the dining surface on a higher plane. When the appliance you want to house in the island is a cooktop, however, safety dictates that the cooktop be on a lower plane, with the snack counter at least four to six inches higher. Specify heat-resistant material for the countertops adjoining the cooktop and at least 24 inches of counter for landing space on both sides, and provide for at least four inches of heat-resistant backsplash.

An island opposite the fridge is a logical place for the microwave. It's still within the work triangle, which makes sense because most of what goes in the microwave comes from the fridge. Alternatively, if your microwave gets more use by the kids as a snack-fixer, you may prefer to locate it outside the triangle but still near the fridge, in a combination work island/snack bar. Wall ovens are often located outside the work triangle since they're not used as much as a cooktop, and anything you bake or roast will stay in the oven for at least 15 minutes. An island may prove the most convenient landing spot for hot foods out of the oven.

In generously sized kitchens, it might be best to think along the lines of "if one island is good, two are better." A primary island may be stationed within the work triangle, housing extra storage, a mini-fridge or refrigerator drawers, a prep sink, a drop-in cooktop, and so on. Another island might serve solely as a snack bar, perhaps with a small TV perched at one end on a swivel base. If this island defines the perimeter of the kitchen, choose your island base, top, and counter stools to coordinate with the decorative scheme of the adjoining room. Whether this means elegant leather bar chairs, pretty wicker with plump cushions, or metal bistro stools with amusing cut-out motifs is up to you. Even in the kitchen, an island is for fun and adventure!

An unusually angled kitchen island allows for deeper drawers where they're needed and makes a dramatic design statement, too. ***Designer: Judy Bakalik, CKD, Heartwood Kitchen & Bath Design. Cabinets: Neff.***

Virtual Solutions à la Carte

There's been a real revolution in the definition of "homework" in the past decade, and today's kitchens have risen to the occasion beautifully. Millions of Americans telecommute from conventional jobs or work independently from home on a part-time or full-time basis. Although a dedicated home office is very popular, another option is to locate the office, or a least a workstation, within the kitchen, so that work can be performed in a common area. Even if the home office is used simply for planning meals and ordering groceries online today, you never know

A quarter-round island offers a clever solution in this clean-lined kitchen. The architectural presence found in the practical butcher-block top and clean white base is echoed in the simply curved, counter-height chairs. ***Designer: Louise A. Gilmartin, Kitchens & Baths.***

Elegant traditional cabinetry combines glass-front, open, and solid-door storage to enclose a corner desk tucked into a kitchen window nook. **Designer: Gerard Ciccarello, CKD, Covenant Kitchens & Baths, Inc. Cabinets: Heritage Custom Kitchens.**

what it might be used for in the future! It would probably be smart to install as sophisticated an electrical system as you can, since your family's needs will likely increase. After all, the kitchen has always been "command central" for the typical family. And, for the many children who have always preferred to do their homework at the kitchen table no matter how well outfitted their rooms, a computer in the kitchen makes it even easier.

For planning menus and paying bills, a narrow countertop extended along a window wall and into the corner makes for an unobtrusive yet roomy desk area in this French country kitchen. **Wallcovering: Seabrook.**

A computer desk in the kitchen can take many forms, but don't just set the electronics onto a base cabinet counter and be done with it. If you spend any time at all at this workstation, you'll need an ergonomically sound chair, plenty of knee space, a keyboard tray that drops down to the correct height, and so on. You may want the workstation to face into the kitchen or into the family room so you can keep an eye on your crew; or you may prefer it tucked into a corner, facing the wall, for a greater sense of privacy. As long as you avoid the busy work triangle area, wherever you can fit in your computer station may work.

Power is what the computerized home is about, so make sure you have enough. You'll probably be adding electrical outlets every 36 inches or so along your backsplashes (or on power strips beneath the upper cabinets if switchplates will disturb your backsplash design), so while the electricity is being planned, plan for the desktop computer area. In addition to a computer and a phone, you may need electrical and phone outlets plus counterspace and lower-storage space for a printer, answering machine, fax machine, and any other "must-have" equipment. To conserve space, look for units that provide more than one of these functions. If this is where you'll stash the small TV, make plans for that, too. All this may mean extra new wiring, but most older homes need it to make the leap into the new electronic era.

Great-looking, tall cupboards flanking a built-in desk with a storage bridge create a practical computer center that fits snugly into a busy kitchen's breakfast area. **Cabinets: Wood-Mode.**

What if you prefer the scenic byway to the electronic highway? Chances are, you'll still be more comfortable with some kind of a workstation, however informal, in the kitchen. Whether you choose a small writing table, a conventional desk to coordinate with the style of your kitchen, or a desk made of the same material as your kitchen is up to you. In a traditional, formal kitchen, you might enjoy an 18th-century "secretaire" that includes upper glassed cabinets and open shelves as well as lower drawers and a drop-down writing surface. In other cases, you'll want to plan upper storage cabinets with either glass or solid doors. You'll need enough counterspace to hold a few desk necessities (pens, notepads, scissors, and so on); a few shallow, wide drawers to stash bills and clutter; and space for your recipe box and the cookbooks you use most. If the desk or counter is tucked into a corner near an adjacent wall or run of tall wood cabinets, you can hang a bulletin board and a good-size calendar.

VIKING

Elements of Design

ON AVERAGE, Americans spend about 16 percent of their kitchen budget on labor; the rest is spent on product. And what product—beautiful, practical, durable, and environmentally responsible! Exciting advances at every budget level are available for today's kitchens, so the sooner you start learning about all your options, the better. It's important to decide exactly what you want before starting work, because changes are costly. So explore the new products, consult with the experts, and take time to specify brands, models, and other details in your contract. Your ultimate kitchen will be made up of all the elements that suit you best.

A high-tech commercial chic kitchen demands modern, up-to-the-minute appliances and accoutrements to complete the look.

Appliances

This commercial-style stainless-steel stove is right at home in a warm, wood-filled French country kitchen where great cuisine rules. ***Designer: Canterbury Design Kitchen Interiors. Stove: Viking; cabinets: Wood-Mode.***

APPLIANCES ARE the workhorses of your kitchen. Together, they will add up to about nine percent of your kitchen budget. This figure is surprisingly low, considering the technological advances and energy efficiencies today's appliances offer. While features and performance are obviously the most important considerations in choosing appliances, how they'll look in your kitchen probably matters to you, too. White appliances are still the classic favorite, followed by black. Stainless steel, with its professional look, continues to grow in popularity. If you covet a simple Shaker-style space or a luxurious Italian villa setting, however, you may want to hide the fridge and dishwasher out of sight. To meet this need, savvy cabinet manufacturers offer coordinated cabinet fronts that adhere easily and provide a custom-designed look. To further the traditional, low-tech look, you can opt for small-appliance depots in countertop-height cabinets. You can even choose a specially designed under-counter oven.

Ovens and Cooktops

The traditional range or stove, a single unit with cooktop above and oven below, is an affordable, space-conserving solution still chosen by most homeowners. But it's just one of the cooking options offered today. Some serious home cooks choose commercial-style stoves with six or eight burners instead of four, basting and grilling functions, and built-in warming ovens. (Real commercial stoves pose special challenges, such as special ventilation systems and noncombustible walls and floors, when used in the home, so commercial-style may be easier to live with.) Other people love the new modular cooktops that let you add burners, downdrafts, griddles, deep-fry and steamer units, woks, rotisseries, and grills. And these are just a few examples of what's available!

A modular approach to overall kitchen design is a pronounced trend. Wall ovens separate from cooktops let you create several cooking work stations instead of just one. A double wall oven stacks two ovens to save space and deliver twice the baking/roasting capacity, which many people find useful for special occasions. And you can still get two-oven stoves, with one oven below the cooking surface and the other well above, at cabinet height.

The first decision in range shopping has always been gas versus electric. Many serious cooks prefer gas for its instant response, precise controllability, and lower operating cost over time. Others praise the evenness of electric heat and the lower initial cost of the appliance. Today, you can get the best of both heating methods with "dual fuel" ranges that let you mix gas and electric heat sources; for example, gas cooktop burners and an electric convection oven/broiler. Convection ovens, most often electric, use heated air to cook up to twice as fast as conventional ovens that rely on radiant heating action. You can even get a combination microwave/convection oven.

Electric coils are the most popular kind of electric burners, and the least costly. Smooth-top surfaces are offered with one of three heat source types: radiating electric coils beneath the glass surface, halogen burners, or magnetic-induction elements. All require thick, flat-bottom cookware. If gas is your choice, sealed burners are easiest to clean, and a pilotless ignition system means no hot spot when burners are off. Commercial-style glass stoves offer high BTUs (British thermal units, the measure of cooking heat) and high style. They require heavy-duty ventilation systems.

What about controls? Controls that are located on the front or on the side of the appliance are most common and convenient, but universal access means just that: While someone in a wheelchair can reach front-situated controls easily, unfortunately, so can a curious toddler. People with young children may prefer controls located on the back-

This clever island design puts the oven right beneath the butcher-block countertop, so you can roll out a pie and pop it in to bake without taking a step. The commercial-style cooktop offers practical storage below. ***Architect: Rolf Kielman, Truex, Cullins & Partners Architects.***

A fully functional range housed in a charming piece of freestanding kitchen furniture is a nostalgic—and very stylish—alternative to built-in cabinets. The airy, unaffected look recalls country kitchens of years ago, with a fresh twist.

splash, out of reach of exploring fingers. Wherever they're located, controls should be easy to understand and operate. Top-of-the-line ovens may include electronic temperature readouts and touch-pad, rather than knob or dial, controls.

While many people like to blend refrigerators and dishwashers into the cabinetry with matching fronts, the latest trend is to keep ranges visible. However, if you do want to de-emphasize your oven, the easiest way is with an under-counter model. (Make sure the oven you choose is designed for under-counter use, because not all are.) You may install a cooktop directly above the oven or locate it elsewhere in the kitchen. A cooktop directly over an under-counter oven functions much the same as a conventional range, but, with no range backsplash and with the control knobs located on the countertop, the result is a more integrated look.

Cleaning baked-on spills from the cooktop has always been a challenge, but several options make short work of them. For easiest cooktop cleaning, consider ranges with ceramic glass cooktops housing electric or halogen burners; simpler knobs and handles; and a top and backsplash constructed from a single piece of metal, so there's no seam to collect spills. Self-cleaning ovens come in two varieties: one that uses a high-heat cycle that turns cooked-on spills into ash you can wipe away, another that offers a continuous-clean function.

Range Hoods

If you don't have a ventilation fan above your cooktop that vents to the attic or outside, you'll want a range hood with ventilation fan built in. Why? Even if you don't find some cooking odors objectionable, vaporized grease can dull beautiful new kitchen surfaces, and moisture can compromise the efficiency of home insulation. The solution is an updraft range hood that funnels cooking grease and smoke into one area so that the fan can draw it through a duct to the outside. Filters capture additional grease and odors. Look for range hoods that come in copper, stainless steel, and other good-looking, easy-care materials, or customize a standard hood with ceramic tile to

Venting an island cooktop is a challenge. This handsome reeded column in wood was the extension this range hood needed to vent through a high ceiling in style.

Showing the famed Italian flair for modern design, this great-looking Euro-style kitchen includes a unique curved range hood that flows smoothly into the backsplash/cooktop/oven unit. **Range hood: Valcucine USA.**

create a major focal point, furthering your decorating scheme. As an alternative, down-draft ventilation, usually part of a cooktop or grill, also employs a fan and duct arrangement. Units that rise above cooktop level provide the most effective venting.

Refrigerators and Freezers

Refrigerators' energy conservation has improved a lot since mandated standards were set in 1993 and 1998. Today's refrigerator-freezer models also offer a lot more convenience. You can still get the basic 18-cubic-foot, freezer-on-top model with wire shelves, but the most popular style offers 20 cubic feet of storage; adjustable glass shelves; meat keeper with temperature control; vegetable crisper with humidity control; ice-maker; and door bins. Next in cost and convenience are models with the freezer located below the refrigerator (a very good option for people with bad backs) and 22-cubic-foot capacity. Side-by-side designs and water- and ice-dispensing "convenience centers" built right into the door add further appeal. Built-in refrigerator-freezers and commercial, stainless-steel models are top-of-the-line choices for luxurious looks or serious, high-volume storage.

How much refrigerator do you need? One rule of thumb says plan on 12 cubic feet for two people and 2 more cubic feet for each additional household member, but other considerations also matter. If you like to stock up during sales, or cook often for crowds, the more room the better. Side-by-side models are easiest to organize, but the smaller models have relatively narrow freezers. Make sure the model you buy can fit a frozen turkey or pizza! In all cooling sections, look for

If you're into gourmet goodies, why not let them show? Going a step beyond glass-door cabinets, this see-through refrigerator door lets you check perishables at a glance.

Now you can tuck a mini-fridge anywhere you can fit a cabinet drawer! Integrated refrigerators and freezers let you store veggies near the sink, fresh fish near the cooktop, leftovers close to the microwave, or milk near the kitchen table. ***Refrigerators: Sub-Zero.***

pull-out, roll-out bins and baskets that make it easy to see everything without having to dig around, squandering energy (yours as well as the refrigerator's!).

Beyond the main fridge, if you've got the room, a separate, under-counter refrigerator for soft drinks and a wine cooling compartment are entertaining options. If you're a serious entertainer, you may want to look into ice makers that fit into the space of a trash compactor and produce large quantities of ice daily.

Sinks and Faucets

You can expect to spend an average of eight percent of your budget on kitchen fixtures and fittings, predominantly on sinks and faucets. Sink shape and size are important, and when checking out a sink's size, pay attention to its depth, too: Bargain sinks may be six or seven inches deep, where eight inches is the standard and ten inches is preferable if you wash a lot of stockpots, pasta pots, and roasters.

Popular kitchen sink configurations include the typical single, large rectangular basin; the double-bowled sink with both sinks the same size for hand-washing and rinsing; or the double-bowled sink with one side considerably smaller, housing the garbage disposer. Three-bowl sinks are also available, in which two larger bowls flank a small, center bowl with the garbage disposer installed; this bowl is often topped with a removable cutting board. In space-challenged kitchens, a pair of matching "corner-square" sinks can make use of an awkward corner and free up straight runs

A corner sink is a great way to make use of space that might otherwise be wasted. This configuration, with two square basins connected at one corner, is especially space-efficient since one basin fits easily on each counter without having to cut the corner and disrupt the cabinets. ***Sink and fixtures: Elkay.***

A classic blue-and-white farmhouse-style kitchen with a taste of Victorian romance features an Old World-style mosaic-tile sink and wall tiles in the color scheme.

of counter for work space. "Corner circle" sinks serve the same function but have a more avant-garde look. A small square or round sink may be used as a vegetable sink in an island or as a bar sink for a wet bar in the great room. Some kitchens also feature a small, shallow, kidney-shaped sink as a second, accessory sink.

Once you choose the shape and size of your sink based on function, your next decision lies in the wide array of available materials. You may opt for a sink in shiny stainless steel, colorful enamel on cast iron, solid surfacing, or quartz composite.

- Stainless steel, a material that has been popular since the 1950s, is sleek, contemporary, and stain resistant. The thickest and most durable steel is 18 gauge; thinner, 20- and 22-gauge steel is more prone to scratches, dents, and even punctures.
- Enamel-on-cast-iron sinks resemble enamel on steel but are more durable and more popular, although the weight of a cast-iron sink requires hefty counters. Enamel sinks come in a wide assortment of colors, including white, the classic favorite, and colors that make a contemporary fashion statement. All have a glasslike surface that's easy to clean, but enamel can chip, revealing black cast iron beneath.
- Solid-surfacing sinks are rimless and are seamlessly fused to the adjacent solid-surfacing counter. A handsome contemporary solution that's relatively easy to clean and repair, solid surfacing offers good color selection and color that goes all the way through. Solid-surfacing sinks cost more than metal ones and require professional installation.
- Quartz composite sinks, a relatively new material, feature color all the way through, good color choices, and the option of a realistic granite look. Like solid surfacing, quartz composite is both stain- and scratch-resistant.

Although kitchen sinks come in a wide variety of shapes, sizes, materials, colors, and configurations, most are mounted to the countertop in one of three ways. In self-rimming sinks, the most common kind, the lip of the sink overhangs the

A roomy double sink and raised gooseneck faucet give this handsome kitchen work area extra elbow room. **Designer: Pamela Bytner, CKD, Bytner Design Associates, Inc. Cabinets: Craft-Maid Custom Kitchens, Inc.**

surface of the countertop on all sides. An integral sink, usually made with solid-surfacing material, is simply a continuation of your countertop. You can also get short-run counters in stainless steel with an integral, stainless-steel sink. The advantage of an integral sink is that it's seamless, with no rim to trap dirt or water. Undermount sinks, another rimless option, feature sink bowls fused to the underside of the counter. This method should not be used with laminate counters but works well with solid surfacing, stone, or stainless steel.

Faucets, handles, and other sink fittings also offer attractive, hard-working options. Separate pull-out sprayers that mount on the sink deck are great for washing large pots or watering plants. You can also get this benefit with some European models in which the faucet head itself is the pull-out sprayer. Euro-style, single-fitting faucets have no bottom plate or deck, unlike U.S. models, and require only one hole in the sink or countertop. American faucets include tall, gooseneck designs that make washing deep pots a breeze. Nice additional features include a lotion/soap dispenser (either or both) and a hot-water dispenser, a small electric heater under the sink that provides 190-degree water.

In faucets and other fittings, you can choose a brushed-nickel finish that's less shiny than classic chrome; or, if you like a modern look, choose white, red, black, or another fashion color enameled on steel. You may even opt for brass made more tarnish-resistant with new titanium-strengthened finishes. For faucet handles, you can choose from wing- or blade-style handles, which can be operated with the back of your wrist, not your hand; easy-to-operate barrel-shaped levers; and knobs or traditional cross-shaped handles. Wing/blade and lever handles are generally considered easiest to grasp and operate, which is an important consideration for those who plan to stay in their home as they age.

Dishwashers

Led by high-end, stainless-steel European models, today's dishwashers are extremely quiet thanks to extra insulation. They're also more energy efficient than they were in the past, using fewer kilowatt-hours per wash cycle, less water, and an air-dry option that doesn't require heat. To further cut energy costs, choose a dishwasher with internal water heating; it increases temperatures to grease-dissolving levels so the machine doesn't place extra demands on your home's hot water heater.

While portable dishwashers are available, most models are built-ins and can be concealed behind panels that match your cabinetry if you desire. Top-of-the-line machines feature electronic touch-pad controls, stainless-steel interiors, and special wash cycles such as crystal, china, and pots/pans. Less-costly models employ push buttons or combine buttons with a dial. These models usually offer three cycles: light, normal, and heavy.

Trash Handling Systems

The question of where to put the trash before it makes its way to the garage or curb is an important one. The best solutions eliminate unsightly, freestanding trash cans or wastebaskets in favor of visually unobtrusive yet easily accessible storage. To make recycling simpler for everyone, find out the separation requirements of your town, then have the right number of recycling bins installed inside a lower cabinet. Consider locating the bins near your kitchen's back door or the door leading out to the garage. If you want to compost organic materials, install a small chute in a counter next to the sink, with a trash receptacle in the cabinet below it.

Disposers

Food waste disposers are considered basic in many kitchen remodelings. Choose either continuous feed, operated by an on/off switch under the sink cabinet or on the wall; or batch feed, activated once the stopper is securely closed and turned. Continuous-feed units are more readily available and less expensive than batch-feed models but are more costly to install. Neither one is "better" than the other; it's a matter of personal choice and preference.

Trash Compactors

Even with today's emphasis on recycling, a trash compactor is useful in reducing the volume of your trash if you're billed by the bag, have to lug bulky, heavy bags out by yourself, or have infrequent pickups and scant trash storage space. Available in 12-, 15- and 18-inch widths, compactors can compress a week's worth of cans (if you don't have recycling) and paper into an easy-to-handle bundle. You'll want to look for a unit with a deodorizing system for odor control plus a lock and key so children aren't able to turn it on. If you would like your compactor to blend in with a run of cabinets, try concealing it behind a matching panel.

Water Purifiers

In the United States, most tap water is safe to drink, but contamination caused by heavy metals, microbes, radon, and industrial and agricultural waste is always a possibility. Carbon filters are the most popular water purifiers, removing residual chlorine, organic chemicals, mercury, and dissolved radon. Many manufacturers offer faucets with filters built right in. Water purification systems are now offered on today's high-end refrigerators to provide clearer, cleaner-tasting ice and water.

According to the National Kitchen & Bath Association (NKBA), most people spend about 52 percent of their kitchen budget on cabinetry, so it pays to do it right. The dominant element in any kitchen, cabinets can be as utilitarian-looking as the appliances around them or as warm and stylish as the rest of the home. There are more than 200 cabinetmakers in the United States alone and scores more in England and Europe, and they each offer a multitude of style options.

For those whose taste in modern reaches the futuristic, this dramatic kitchen gets its kicky flair from a spaceship-inspired backsplash and cabinets with stiletto-heeled stainless-steel feet. **Cabinets: Valcucine USA.**

Cabinets come in two main varieties—stock, or mass-produced to standard size specifications, and custom, which are made to order for your kitchen. Some makers offer "stock custom" options; a wider range of stock choices with modifiable elements you can mix and match to create custom solutions. To estimate the cost of the new cabinetry you've chosen, your installer will determine the number of wall cabinets, base cabinets, and specialty units (pantry-type cupboards, lazy Susans, appliance garages, open shelving, and so on).

Cabinet Exteriors

Cabinet styles and materials come in numerous varieties. For a sleek, contemporary look, you might explore European frameless cabinets, cabinets with brushed metal inserts, or cool, laminate cabinets in solid colors or faux stone patterns. Plain fronts and simple (or outrageously inventive) door and drawer pulls seal the look. For lovers of traditional style, raised-panel cabinets are classics; arched-top "cathedral" panel cabinets are especially elegant. Traditional hardware may be as simple as plain wood, Shaker-style pulls or as elaborate as Chippendale-style brass handles.

Beyond the options available in cabinet door and drawer styles and hardware, you also can modify your contemporary or traditional look with formal or casual finishes. Dark mahogany or cherry finishes bespeak formality, whether the style is modern or 18th century. Pine is a perennial, casual favorite. Naturally finished maple is on the semiformal side due to its fine grain; naturally finished oak's prominent grain makes it definitely casual. Any wood given a bisque, or whitewashed, finish is casual in a romantic sort of way.

Perhaps the most classic solution is cabinetry painted gloss white. This look can lean toward either formal or casual, depending on hardware and accessories. And don't forget about colorfully painted cabinet sections; they're a great way to further your scheme and create the European look of freestanding kitchen furniture. (To really give practical built-in cabinets the freestanding look, choose cabinets with toe-kick spaces and furniture feet.)

New cabinets are most often the solution in kitchen remodelings, but if your old cabinet interiors are in good condition and you like your kitchen's layout, you may decide to simply reface your existing cabinets for about half the cost of purchasing entirely new cabinets. The process basically involves installing new doors and drawer fronts and applying coordinating surface veneers to all visible exterior areas. Some companies reface only with laminates; others offer a limited array of woods as well. Most cabinet refacing companies can build additional custom units to match the refaced units.

This clean-lined modern kitchen gives '50s funk a jump start: Sliding-door cabinets sport mottled glass with a retro, frost-etched look.

Solid-door cabinets aren't your only choice, especially in today's freestanding-look kitchens. While an unbroken line of upper cabinets is a contemporary favorite, many people like the variety open shelves and glass-front cabinets provide. Glass doors come with mullions (wood dividers) in traditional styles. A word of caution: Open shelves are a popular part of today's kitchen look, but the combination of airborne cooking grease and everyday dust can mean more dusting and wiping than many people would like. For an open look without this drawback, consider glass-door cabinets. Or, if you really want open shelves, opt for dust-hiding, midtone colors or wood tones and an easy-to-clean, glossy surface.

Arts and Crafts style combines the artistry of hand-painted cabinets in soft tones of blue with the honest good looks of naturally finished oak cabinets. **Cabinets: Mark Wilkinson Furniture, Ltd.**

Rustic knotty pine makes a great cabinet hutch that stores the microwave oven and includes a garage for mixers and other small appliances. **Designer: Joan Viele, CKD, Kitchen Dimensions.**

Cabinet Interiors

You can magnify the storage space of any cabinetry with savvy interior fittings. One of the best is a corner cabinet fitted with a lazy Susan to provide 360-degree access to supplies. Appliance depots or garages—often with sliding, hinged, or tambour (roll-top) doors—keep mixers, toasters and other small appliances dust-free and out of sight. The best compartments are fitted with outlets for the added convenience of using the appliances right there where they are. European-style spice drawers at counter height help you avoid the common error of storing fragile flavors above the heat source. Deep drawers also work for stashing unsightly but necessary items like a garbage bin or household cleaners. In fact, any time you can use a pull-out drawer rather than an unfitted cupboard, you'll do well; especially for cookpots and other heavy items. Produce bins keep fresh fruits and vegetables out of sight behind closed doors but well ventilated for a longer shelf life. Deep, narrow spaces, fitted as slide-out cabinets, are perfect for big pan lids, cookie sheets, and other unwieldy items.

Outside, it's traditional pickled wood with a faux door and drawer; inside, it's a convenient pull-out unit with four spacious shelves. **Designer: Kimball Derrick, CKD, K. D. and Steele Cabinetry.**

How does one keep sharp knives and unsightly trash and recycling bins accessible but out of the way? This slotted knife drawer and deep, two-section trash drawer are savvy solutions. The pull-out cutting boards offer extra work space, too.

Storage doesn't get any more inventive than this: Small, see-through compartments with measuring cup–type pull handles keep staples at eye level in the food prep area. It's extremely practical and makes a visually pleasing design statement, too.

Other Storage

POT RACKS and plate racks are charming, open ways to store good-looking kitchen items. Even if your kitchen's never had a pantry, or if you, like many homeowners, have appropriated the pantry space to create a larger kitchen, you can still have the benefits via a pantry wall. This storage system offers floor-to-ceiling storage for packaged and canned goods on shelves behind double doors or in a series of cupboards. Many pantry-style cupboards have plastic-covered vinyl racking installed in the doors for extra storage. Above-cabinet storage for baskets and little-used, large cooking utensils is a practical and attractive solution for those who don't mind dusting them when they are taken down from storage. And don't forget about tall, narrow cabinetry for storing brooms and mops, plus overhead shelving to keep household cleaners away from children and pets.

An over-the-counter pot rack and crown-molded shelves provide extra storage space in a small kitchen as well as add interesting detail to a traditional look. ***Wallcovering: FSC Wallcoverings.***

Ingenious base cabinets with wood-framed glass fronts evoke an Old World charm while conveniently keeping levels of pasta, beans, and other dry goods in clear sight.

Flexible storage creates a visually interesting, practical kitchen with contemporary pizzazz. This modern Euro-style system hangs shiny cooking utensils within open shelving and encloses dishes behind attractive cobalt-blue and beechwood grid cupboards. Pull-out drawers and bins add to the flexibility. ***Cabinets: Valcucine USA.***

ABOUT 11 PERCENT of your kitchen budget will be used for countertops. Counters offer a great opportunity to create a fashion statement, and the price ranges are as varied as the styles. Whatever your preferences, rounded corners on countertops are a smart move for safety's sake. For the sake of your budget as well as for specific performance needs, feel free to mix several different countertop materials in different areas of the kitchen.

Mixing countertop materials is a practical and attractive option. Marble works great for pastry-making, but you don't need a glossy stone surface on which to unload grocery bags or pile up dirty dinner dishes. Butcher block is warm, but you don't want it next to the sink, where it might get water damaged. You like the elegant look of granite, but it's a bit out of your price range for a whole kitchen. So why not mix and match?

Today's kitchen design trends favor the warmth and character created by mixing stone (or faux stone) and wood counters in different areas. You might choose butcher block or marble for the counter on which you plan to prep vegetables or roll out pastry, while solid surfacing is used for other countertops. And you might want to use real granite on a high-visibility kitchen island with coordinating faux granite laminate on perimeter counters. Most natural materials now have attractive synthetic alternatives that incorporate photographic reproductions of "the real thing," so countertops at every price point look better than ever. Take a look at your options.

Custom edges in solid surfacing or wood are a natural for countertops when you want the unlimited color range of laminate counters but don't want the telltale black edging. This kitchen uses a sharp combination of black, almond, and white in varying amounts to create an eye-catching, tailored design accent. **Laminate: Wilsonart.**

LAMINATE

Economical and good-looking, laminates consist of layers of decorative paper sandwiched together and laminated with a patterned paper on top, all bonded to a particle-board countertop surface. From elegant faux-marble and granite looks to fun and funky, '50s boomerang designs, laminates respond to every fashion look. Laminates have good stain, abrasion, and moisture resistance, but scratches and nicks do show and can't be repaired. (An all-over pattern on the dark side minimizes visible marks, and color-through laminates show less evidence of wear.) You'll also need to protect laminate counters from hot pots, which can cause irreparable scorches and even melting. Specify a rolled edge or another color of laminate trim on the counter's edge to eliminate the black edging line between the two planes.

Solid Surfacing

Nonporous, seamless surfaces are made of a blend of acrylic and/or polyester resins with mineral fillers for a smooth feel that's similar to natural stone, but not as cool to the touch. Available in solid colors and in faux-stone patterns, solid surfacing is easy to clean and maintain; burns or stains often can be repaired or buffed away. This material is also more workable than stone: Contrasting colors and shapes can be pieced together for a custom design; the material can be routed for elegant edge designs. An integral solid-surfacing sink is an appealing and practical option. Solid-surfacing material comes with impressive warranties when installed by a professional fabricator.

Ceramic Tile

Made of high-fired clay with a baked-on colored surface, ceramic tile resists stains, water, and heat and will last a lifetime with normal care. It also offers endless custom-colored options, including luxurious hand-painted designs to coordinate with any motif. As with any surface cut into tiles rather than in slabs, you'll have to contend with cleaning grout, but today's cleaners make short work of that task. Some grouts have been treated with mildewcides, and the current trend toward midtone grout means less visible staining. You can also ask that tiles be laid close together to reduce grout line maintenance. Like natural stone surfacing materials, tile is not resilient, so it's tough on dropped glassware.

A small kitchen dazzles with lively, ethnic flair thanks to Moorish-inspired ceramic tiles in cheerful primary colors cut with white. **Designer: Joan Viele, CKD, Kitchen Dimensions.**

Wood

Practical, naturally warm, and handsome, wood can be finished, left unfinished, or periodically refinished. Because wood is susceptible to warping and cracking from moisture, wood countertops are most often made of butcher block (many small, thick pieces of wood glued together). Wood is also susceptible to stains and burns and, because it's

Not every home can boast a kitchen with a skylit, vaulted ceiling and a fieldstone wall, but affordable, handsome butcher-block countertops are within easy reach for everyone. **Architect: Charles Cunniffe, Charles Cunniffe Architects.**

porous, should be regularly cleaned with an antibacterial cleaner. (Many people feel more comfortable cutting raw meats on a nonporous cutting board.) For a low-sheen surface, you should order your wood countertop without a gloss sealant, and plan on preserving it with an occasional mineral oil application, rubbed in well. For a glossier look, specify a polyurethane-finished surface.

Marble and Granite

Marble and granite are the luxury choices of surfacing material and can easily last a lifetime or longer. Highly polished, smooth-edged stone costs more than unpolished surfaces and rough-hewn edges, but the smoother the countertop is, the easier it is to keep clean. Marble's cool, smooth surface is perfect for making pastry, but it is porous and can be stained, so regular care and sealing (with salad oil in food prep area, commercial sealer elsewhere) is important. Granite is much less porous than marble but can be stained by grease. Granite doesn't scratch, and chips on the corners can be repaired. Thickness of the countertop greatly affects the price. If it's in your budget, specify your slab stone 1¼-inch deep, so it's strong enough to survive shipment and fabrication and sturdy enough to be used as an unsupported ½-inch counter overhang.

Usually installed in counter-length slabs, natural stone is also available in somewhat less durable tile form for easier installation and lower cost. Since the quarrying and finishing of many running feet in a single slab is what makes stone countertops so expensive, smaller pieces can help make stone more affordable. As with ceramic tile, have your marble or granite tiles laid close together to eliminate grout line maintenance.

Granite isn't just for countertops, as this posh "Baltic Brown" granite backsplash proves. For added drama, custom mosaic inset squares of contrasting marble and granite were installed. **Designer: Gary White, CKD, CBD, CID, Kitchen & Bath Design.**

Modern style here pairs rich wood tones with sharp, shiny black. Dramatic downlights bring the look to life and make the cook's work easier, too.

YOU'D THINK a room in which sharp knives and boiling liquids are used would get serious attention when it comes to visibility, but lighting is often one of the last considerations in kitchen design. In too many kitchens, a central ceiling fixture leaves the cook working in his/her own shadow, for example. Others feature enough fixtures but not enough wattage. One of the challenges is that poor lighting is hard for the average person to detect; the kitchen just may not "feel right." If your family didn't tend to congregate in your old kitchen, look at this renovation as a chance to see the space in a whole new light.

A lighting plan for your kitchen requires the same elements as for any other room. You'll need the right mix of ambient (overall) lighting to illuminate the space; task lighting to provide illumination for specific activities; mood lighting to create atmosphere; and accent lighting to draw attention to special collections or artwork. If yours is a multipurpose kitchen that opens to adjacent rooms, it's especially important for light to adapt to a wide variety of situations: cooking, dining, entertaining, or just relaxing in softly lit repose while life goes on in a neighboring space. What's required? More variety in light fixtures, both decorative and concealed; and dimmers (rheostats) on every light switch. In addition to ceiling-mounted fixtures, many people choose to install strip lights under every upper cupboard that has a work surface counter below. The effect is dramatic as well as very practical.

Lighting Types

Fluorescent lighting tubes, a favorite during the post-WWII era of "kitchens-as-sanitary-labs," fell out of favor in later decades. Fluorescent lamps (the replaceable bulbs or tubes) are costlier to buy than incandescent bulbs, but they cost significantly less to operate, which is why they're still used so extensively in commercial settings. Fluorescent fixtures are energy efficient, throwing off much less heat than halogen or incandescent bulbs, but the resultant light is cool, too. The effect may be "cold," with a blue-green cast that's at odds with the warm, hospitable ambience you'd like for a kitchen. Recent improvements have made more natural, "warm white" fluorescent lighting available.

Incandescent bulbs, the most common residential lighting source, impart a warmer, more yellow light but, at the same time, heat up the room more. These bulbs are widely available and come in a broad range of wattages, tints, and sizes to fit virtually any style of lighting fixture, whether it's traditional or contemporary.

Attractive suspended fixtures make this great island even more of a focal point as well as adding needed task lighting.

Halogen lights, the most recent development, create intensely bright, sunshine-quality light from a relatively small bulb source. Halogen bulbs are costly, however, and must be used with great care. Because they generate such intense heat, these bulbs pose a greater fire hazard than other lighting types and should not be used near kitchen curtains or where they may come into contact with plastic materials.

Contemporary and retro-style kitchens take naturally to fluorescent lights, including whimsical neon-colored options. Traditional-style kitchens fit easily with warm incandescent light, and all styles are at home with halogen, which most closely mimics daylight.

Lighting Fixtures

The options are practically limitless. Contemporary fixtures in chrome and colored glass are often simple and Space Age inspired, hanging like jewels in the functional space. Traditional fixtures go beyond the ubiquitous stained-glass pendant lamp to include classical sconces, green glass-and-brass banker's lamps, white hobnailed milkglass shades, and more. Halophane lamps, evolved from vintage warehouse fixtures, bridge traditional and modern looks; their ribbed-glass globes create a soft light with a chic profile.

To supplement bigger fixtures, hanging halogen lamps, which use tiny, low-voltage bulbs, make big lighting possible with very unobtrusive fixtures. For contemporary-style kitchens, track lights with incandescent or halogen bulbs combine spotlights with floodlights and let you aim the light wherever you choose. Recessed spotlights or floodlights are the most unobtrusive choice and provide excellent ambient and task lighting, but they are costlier to install because they require cutting holes in the ceiling. If they're an option, recessed lights may be your best bet if your goal is today's light levels with yesterday's charm.

KITCHEN FLOORING will cost an average of four percent of your kitchen budget, and, given the stress a major remodeling puts on the floor, you can count on spending a little extra to get your floor into shape. In general, lighter-colored flooring of any kind makes a room seem larger, as does laying tiles on the diagonal rather than parallel to the walls. Larger tiles, 12×12 inches and up, are at home in contemporary-style kitchens and have the advantage of minimizing grout lines. Some traditional looks work best with smaller tiles; small tiles are also what you'll need if you want to design patterned floors or borders.

This romantic French country kitchen carries artistry and charm right down to the floor, which features a rich malachite-green tile pattern with "feathers" dropped randomly on top for a whimsical trompe l'oeil effect.

Vinyl

Available in sheets or tiles, vinyl is today's most popular kitchen flooring because it's durable, easy to install, easy to maintain, and inexpensive compared to most other flooring materials. On the fun side, vinyl also offers the greatest range of styles at a price, from '50s boomerang motifs to ancient Roman marble tiles. Better-quality vinyl flooring features "inlaid construction" with color and pattern uniform throughout rather than printed on top, for richer color and less noticeable nicks. Top-of-the-line vinyl floors have a thick urethane wear layer that offers the most shine and shine retention, as well as the greatest stain resistance. Mid-range vinyl may also offer a urethane wear layer, but it won't be as thick; lower-range vinyl has a vinyl wear layer that's best for households without pets and kids. Sheet vinyl, best installed by a professional, eliminates tile lines or possible lift-up due to standing water. Vinyl tiles with self-stick backs can be easily and quickly installed by just about any homeowner. Tiles also let you design patterns or borders using several colors.

Linoleum

A leading kitchen flooring material until after World War II, when America fell in love with plastic, linoleum is staging a comeback. An environmentalist's delight, linoleum is made of all natural products—linseed oil, pine resin, and wood flour. Inexpensive and durable, today's linoleum comes in matte-finished solid colors and marbleized patterns. It is ideal for retro-style kitchens, especially those striving for a 1920s to 1950s feel. It is also a very affordable option for people with lower budgets.

LAMINATE

One of the newer synthetic flooring options, laminate flooring looks like wood, stone, or marble because the pattern is actually a photograph of the "real thing." Laminate flooring is made of multiple layers of material including a super-hard plastic top layer over a layer with a photographic imprint of wood or stone. It's many, many times more wear-resistant than countertop laminates and can usually be laid directly over an existing floor. Proper installation is crucial. Although laminate can be installed by a savvy do-it-yourselfer, it is best handled by an experienced pro.

Cherry hardwood flooring imparts natural warmth and luxury to this timeless kitchen accented with black granite countertops and black glass tile backsplash. ***Designers: Deborah MacNair, CKD, and Greta Burandt, Thurston Kitchen and Bath, Inc.***

WOOD

Hardwood kitchen floors can last a lifetime and harmonize with just about any kitchen decor. Warm, natural, and resilient, wood floors only gain charm and character with life's inevitable nicks and dents. Rustic oak, with its pronounced grain, is great for casual or country traditional-style kitchens; fine-grained maple and cherry create richly elegant looks; ash, beech, and birch are sleek and modern. Other handsome favorites include hickory, pecan, walnut, mahogany, and teak. Soft woods, most often pine, have a country-style charm but do show wear and damage more than hardwoods.

Wood flooring comes in several forms.

- Plank flooring features boards three to seven inches wide and three-quarters of an inch thick that are cut to lengths up to about eight feet. Wide planks show off the grain of the wood and are associated with traditional looks, especially when wood dowels, plugs, or decorative nails are used to anchor the boards.
- Strip flooring features narrow boards (under three inches wide). Versatile and attractive, strip flooring works for both casual and formal, traditional and modern rooms. Ideally, boards should run parallel to the room's long axis. Using only "shorts" (boards shorter than 18 inches) makes a room look larger. Special effects can be created with borders of different woods.
- Parquet is patterned wood flooring made of $\frac{5}{16}$-inch-thick geometric shapes puzzled together

When the mood is sophisticated and expansive, nothing beats the elegance of a beautifully polished wood floor, here opening the kitchen into a great room with the same flooring.

to create larger pieces about eight- to twelve inches square. Of course, more pieces mean more opportunities for moisture to seep in and warp or loosen flooring, but with its multidirectional patterns, parquet is less likely than strip or plank flooring to draw attention to a floor with irregular dimensions.

While historic purists advocate natural oil treatments to resist moisture and staining, most people today choose a polyurethane, moisture-cure urethane, or waterbased urethane finish. Some wood floors are given an aged, distressed finish at the factory or after installation; for authentically aged floors, some homeowners seek out dismantled barn planks to plane and install as flooring.

Decorative Wood Floor Effects

In addition to natural-woodtone stains, wood floors take nicely to colorwash stains that let the grain show. They also take well to painting. Chic and classic looks include stripes, checkerboard squares, or diamonds using two alternating-color stripes. Faux-stone looks are also classic options and may be combined with checkerboard squares or diamonds: During the colonial period, itinerant artists were hired to paint plain wood floors in such faux marble tile patterns. Spatter-painted wood floors featuring solid-color grounds flecked with dots of many other colors are a charming, surprisingly modern look with origins in colonial times.

Floor stenciling, another traditional favorite, takes much of its character from the color choice: medium blue with red, pink, white, and black for Pennsylvania Dutch style; goldenrod, hunter-green, spice-brown, and rust for Mission/Arts and Crafts style; and so on. Stencil motifs also flag certain styles: stylized hearts and birds for Pennsylvania Dutch and acorns and oak leaves for Mission, for example. Lately, stencils of scrolls, regal insignia, and other elegant European motifs have found their way onto American wood floors, too. Rendered in oil paint and protected with polyurethane finish, these artful floors can last a long time.

Rubber Flooring

A popular flooring in health-care, restaurant, and other commercial settings, rubber floors are an ingenious solution for creating commercial-style kitchens at home. Among the most resilient and comfortable floorings to walk and stand on, rubber floors are easy to clean and are extremely forgiving of dropped glassware. Offered in textured sheets or tile, rubber floors may last 20 years.

Ceramic Tile

A decorative building material since ancient times, ceramic tile retains its colorful charm virtually forever. Made of clay that is pressed, glazed, and fired, ceramic tile has many stonelike qualities: It stands up easily to hot pots and is cool to the touch, but it is tough on dropped glassware. Ceramic wears for ages but, like stone, can chip or crack under heavy abuse. Colors and designs are literally unlimited. In addition to a vast selection of beguiling patterns, you can custom-order tiles that are hand-painted with color schemes and motifs you personally specify to coordinate with your kitchen. High-gloss finishes make it easy to wipe splatters from countertops and walls, but for floors, it's safer to select matte or textured-glazed tiles to reduce slipping when the surface is wet. To minimize grout discoloration from mildew and food stains, specify a grout with mildewcide in the mixture or a midtone grout (taupe and gray are practical and popular), and use a mild bleach cleaner.

Rugged flagstone gives an outdoor ambience and echoes mountain views with the matchless dignity of stone.
Architect: Charles Cunniffe, Charles Cunniffe Architects.

Quarry and Terra-Cotta Tiles

Rustic and handsome, quarry tile is a mix of clay, shale, or earth extruded to produce an unglazed tile. Terra-cotta (literally "baked earth") tile is made of clay that's been fired but left unglazed. Some terra-cotta tiles come with a baked-on sealer; other terra-cotta tiles and quarry tiles should be sealed to prevent permanent staining. These tiles may also be glazed for more lustrous color and a more refined look.

Natural Stone Tiles

Limestone, tumbled marble, and slate tiles are among the most elegant flooring choices available. These tiles share properties with marble, granite, and other stone materials, but are valued as much for their interesting textures as for their colorations. Natural stone tiles must be sealed to prevent stains.

WHETHER OR NOT there's a lot of kitchen wall space left on view after the new cabinets and appliances are in place, you'll want your walls to support your decorating scheme. If your kitchen redo involves more decorating than remodeling, you'll be pleased at how much of an improvement new wall treatments can make. Coordinate the wall treatment style and color with your cabinets, or, if your cabinets aren't being replaced, consider painting them to match the new wall color. Either way, you'll cool the clutter and create a more spacious, calming look, whatever your style.

Here, a rustic brick-red and blue dining nook is enriched by vibrantly colored upper walls and the extra textural appeal of tiled light blue wainscoting—a perfect complement to the natural wood tones of the table, chairs, and cozy bench. The brick column adds to the rustic feel.

PAINT

Paint is the kitchen wall treatment that's easiest to change, easiest to clean, and least expensive. Many experts recommend "eggshell" paint (paint with a slight sheen) for walls and semigloss paint for trim in homes without kids and pets, and semigloss walls and high-gloss trim for homes that need to endure more wear and tear. All the usual recommendations about paint effects apply to kitchen paint. Light colors dry lighter and dark colors dry darker than they appear when wet, so buy a small amount and test it on your wall before making a commitment to gallons. Light colors will make your kitchen look more spacious and cool; midtone and dark colors will make it look cozier and warmer. Traditional styles usually feature white or other contrast-color trim; contemporary styles feature walls and trim of the same color. If you plan to use both wallcovering and paint in your kitchen, choose the wallcovering first. It's much easier to custom-mix a paint to match a wallcovering than it is to find a wallcovering containing the exact color of your paint!

Don't overlook the elegant potential of special faux-finish effects with paint. Sponging and ragging, for example, can create a sense of airiness or rustic charm. A breakfast nook or pantry door is a great place to create a sense of vista with a classic trompe l'oeil still life or garden scene.

WALLCOVERING

If you want a more complex color scheme or pattern than paint makes possible, or if your walls are in less-than-paint-perfect condition, wallcoverings offer dimension, warmth, and eye appeal with surprisingly easy care. Modern kitchen wallcoverings bear little resemblance to fragile wallpapers of yore. They're also a world away from the less-than-inspiring looks that used to be available in coated wallpapers for the kitchen. Today, kitchen wallcoverings are as beautiful and subtle as traditional wallpapers for other rooms, but they're not just spongeable, they're scrubbable.

Go with the faux: Specialty wall treatments don't have to come from paint. Wallcoverings make it easy to bring the casual elegance of faux finishes to today's kitchens. ***Wallcovering: Seabrook Wallcoverings, Inc.***

Traditional-style rooms are made for wallcoverings, and you can find motifs inspired by just about every historical period, each in a wide selection of colors. Many wallcovering companies offer carefully researched collections that are adaptations of actual historic wallpapers, recolored for today's tastes. Others replicate the colors as well as the patterns of historical papers, if you're really intent on a historically correct impression. And, while paint is generally less expensive than paper, if you want a trompe l'oeil picture, it's probably going to be much less costly to purchase a length of scenic paper than it would be to commission a painting.

Modern rooms don't have to do without wallcoverings, either. In addition to nostalgic motifs from the 1920s–1950s, wallcoverings that simulate sponging, marbling, stippling, and other timeless faux-finishing techniques are plentiful. While rooted in ancient techniques, these styles work beautifully in contemporary kitchens.

Paneling

From rustic, cabin-style kitchens to elegant European kitchens, wood paneling can create a mood like no other wall treatment. Unless your kitchen gets lots of natural light and is on the large side, you probably will want to keep the wood tones on the naturally pale side. Whitewashed wood is a great compromise if you want a beachside or cottage look; it delivers the warmth of wood and the space-expanding qualities of white. Like other wallcoverings, paneling is a fine solution for less-than-perfect wall surfaces, providing dimension, warmth, and subtle visual interest. Wood paneling upkeep is much the same as for cabinets, and natural wood tones have the advantage of hiding fingerprints and smudges.

THE CLASSIC CHARM of café curtains is often associated with kitchen window treatments, but these aren't the only choice. Fabric valances make pleasing toppers to café sets and are great for traditional and retro decorating schemes. Roman shades are chic solutions for neoclassical or contemporary spaces. Metal mini-blinds are also fine in modern rooms and have the added advantage of furthering any color scheme and being more fire resistant than other window treatments. Matchstick or bamboo shades are a novel approach that adds an especially pleasing touch in kitchens showcasing an ethnic flair. In natural tones, they offer the plus of hiding dust.

This kitchen employs a light touch at the windows, with appealing results. Shirred white lace café-length curtains provide a measure of privacy without blocking the light. Elaborate painted "ribbons" create a unique border.

You may decide on an elaborate treatment in an eat-in area, but it's best to keep fabrics, tassels, and such well away from the cooking arena. For a dramatic look without a lot of drape, consider pelmets (hard valances jigsawed out of thin wood) to frame your windows. If your kitchen opens into a great room or family room, try coordinating the window treatments. They don't need to match, but they should relate. If your family room draperies are patterned in blue and gold, for example, consider a honey-hued bamboo shade or a solid blue mini-blind for the kitchen. If you've got elaborate burgundy floral draperies in the great room, think about a burgundy plaid in the kitchen, and line or trim the great room draperies with a bit of the plaid. In general, keep kitchen wallcoverings a bit simpler than those in adjoining rooms.

Vividly colored and simply styled, these scarlet-and-gold striped café curtains hang from rings. The colors are echoed in the fabrics of the smaller towels and the funky, custom kitchen tiles that ring the room. ***Wallcovering: Raymond Waites Manor Collection, FSC Wallcoverings.***

THE MORE YOUR kitchen is the heart of your home, the more important it is to get the windows and doors right. Good windows aren't cheap, but they're a home improvement whose cost can be offset over time due to energy savings. If you spend a lot of time in the kitchen, you'll want windows that let in the great outdoors—not ones that make you feel shut away. And if your guests are as likely to come in through the back as through the front, you'll want doors that work well in addition to looking good. If your kitchen is off the garden, you may want an additional set of French doors for easy accessibility.

When the view is great, an array of windows arranged like a picture wall is a modern way to take it all in. Interior spaces get a dash of brightness from deftly placed skylights.

In general, look at your kitchen remodeling as a chance to bring in more natural light, either with bigger windows or with windows that have greater glass-to-sash ratios. Today's window technology lets you get more light without sacrificing energy efficiency, and security systems can increase your options for more windows.

Windows

Windows may be custom, semicustom, or stock, but they're all constructed to fit snugly in the window opening provided. You can choose from aluminum, vinyl, wood, aluminum over wood, and vinyl over wood, depending on your needs and budget. Whatever material you prefer, the best news about double- or triple-pane windows is that separate storm windows are a thing of the past.

- Aluminum is the most economical material but may conduct cold, heat, and moisture. It's maintenance free, but if you elect to paint it, it requires yearly maintenance like any other painted outdoor surface on your home.
- Vinyl is also maintenance free and cannot usually be painted successfully, but it comes in a range of popular trim colors as well as in white.
- Wood, the classic window frame material, is still favored for many high-end and historic homes.

Although its insulating capacity is unsurpassed, wood needs regular repainting in order to retard rotting from standing moisture and other weather damage.

Many people feel aluminum- or vinyl-clad wood offers the best combination of insulation and weather resistance, but up close, it may be apparent that the surface is not wood.

Style Choices

- **Double-hung.** The most common kitchen window is the classic double-hung unit that slides up and down and provides a minimum of 50 percent ventilation. It's difficult to operate when situated over a counter or sink and is not a good idea over a cooktop. Double-hung windows are the preferred style for traditional kitchens and may be required in historic homes. Real wood muntins (dividing bars) that create true divided lites are significantly costlier but look much better, even at a distance, than etched-on, faux dividers or snap-in grills. Look for double-hung windows that swing in for easy cleaning from inside your home (especially useful for windows above the ground floor).
- **Sliders.** Modern alternatives to double-hungs include sliders, which operate like sliding doors on horizontal tracks. Above a countertop or sink, they're a bit easier to use than double-hungs.
- **Casement.** More common than double-hungs are casement windows, which are actually an older, simpler style than double-hungs. Casement windows are hinged on the side and can swing in or out to provide complete ventilation. They usually operate with crank handles, making them easy to operate, even when placed above counters and sinks. Make sure your casements are hinged to swing outward, or you'll need to allow space in front of the window for opening.
- **Decorative Windows.** Decorative windows are available in many shapes and sizes, but among the most pleasing is the half-round, sometimes called Palladian after the classic architect Palla-

A rounded breakfast nook gets the star treatment with double-height windows: garden-level windows and arched Palladian-style upper windows. All windows enjoy the luxury of true divided lites. **Design: Tidmore-Henry & Associates.**

In a luxuriously appointed kitchen, a vaulted glass ceiling expands the sense of spaciousness while letting in even more light. White skylight window frames enhance the open-to-outdoors feeling.

This three-section window merits an unusual treatment, helping to draw even more attention to the half-round window above the center section.

dio, who popularized them. Half-round windows can be positioned above doors, above other windows, or in shallow wall spaces to bring in more light and create architectural interest. Quarter-round and elliptical versions are also available.

Doors

Glazed doors let in the light, but they also pose a greater security issue than solid doors. Sliding doors are contemporary classics, at home in modern or retro rooms. They allow easy access to patios and decks and eliminate the need to sacrifice floor space for door swing. For a romantic traditional look, French doors are the style of choice. These hinged, swinging doors traditionally are used in pairs and open from the center. If possible, they should open to the inside, although this does require allotting door-swing space.

Glazing

No matter what types of glazed windows and doors you select, you need to consider the actual glazing used. In all but the most temperate climates (where there's little need during the year for heating or air conditioning), double-glazing—two panes of glass with an air space between—should be the minimum standard. Double-glazing provides an insulating value of R-2, versus R-1 for single glazing. Even more energy-efficient, but only slightly more expensive, is low-E glazing. In this system, a microscopically thin metallic film or coating is applied to the panes during double-glazing. The coating selectively transmits and reflects different energy wavelengths, boosting R value to between 3 and 4; the higher ratings are achieved by using argon gas in the space between the panes of glass.

As an added benefit, low-E glazing inhibits the transmission of ultraviolet light, reducing the danger of furnishings fading or sun-rotting due to direct, daily exposure. In hot climates, consider glazing that combines low-E technology with tinted glass to substantially reduce solar heat gain and air conditioning costs. Window technology now offers two low-E films in "super" windows with a rating as high as R-8.

Hardware

KITCHEN HARDWARE—window cranks and pulls, cabinet knobs and handles, door and drawer pulls, and more, are often called the jewelry of the room. They don't have to match, and, in most cases, you *won't* be able to match them. But do keep the number of different looks to a minimum. For example, don't mix shiny brass, brushed brass, chrome, brushed nickel-finish steel, white-enameled metal, and so on, all in one room. Rather, pick two or three colors/finishes and stick with them, and keep in mind any hardware visible from an adjoining great room or family room. You'll want to stay with a complementary look.

In general, bright and brushed/antiqued brass hardware are considered elegant traditional, nickel-finish steel is traditional, wrought iron or wood is rustic traditional, and shiny chrome and enameled steel are modern. However, shape can also affect whether a particular metal "reads" modern or classic. You have more choices than you may think.

Use hardware to personalize your kitchen. If you don't like the standard knobs that came with your stock cabinets, shop for novelty ones you like better. Why settle for a plain chrome knob when you can have a knob or pull that's an antiqued brass acorn, a verdigris frog, or a pewter-look miniature fork? After all, creating a new and improved kitchen may be work, but you can still have fun and indulge your taste. That's what a kitchen should be all about!

Simple pulls in stainless steel unify cabinets in two different wood tones and help tie this kitchen together with one simple look.

Just because a decorating scheme is busy and lively doesn't mean little details like hardware can be neglected. In this colorful kitchen, the red door and drawer pulls add to the charm of the vivid room.

In a kitchen with south-of-the-border pizzazz, silvertone Mexican concha buckles are the perfect hardware accents. Today, kitchen cabinet drawer and door pulls can be found in just about any shape and finish to suit your fancy.

Design Ideas

IS YOUR IDEA of the ultimate kitchen elegantly traditional, excitingly modern, warmly nostalgic, or creatively eclectic? While kitchens come in all shapes and sizes, one thing's sure: Whatever decorating style you love, you can make it work in today's kitchen without sacrificing a bit of performance or style. Whether you plan to build an ambitious new design from the ground up or just want to refresh and update your existing space, you can indulge in your favorite design signatures—and create a one-of-a-kind kitchen that expresses your individuality, too. When you browse these pages, you'll see how today's kitchens can be beautiful *and* easy to live with.

Free-form design, bright colors, and modern elements are right at home in a contemporary-style kitchen.

American Country

TIMELESSLY APPEALING, American country carries the spirit of an age when the family farmhouse was the heart of an ever-growing nation. The American country look was started by colonists in the 1600s. Region by region, decade by decade, the style adapted and changed, taking on new interpretations and elements with each new generation. What's basic? Warm, natural tones: wheat, wood, weathered brass and pewter, antiqued ivory-white. For accent colors, choose rich but soft tones: wine-red, paprika, denim-blue, mustard-gold, and teal-green the shade of a mallard's wing. In fabric, you'll see simple patterns, with patchwork, pieced from store-bought scraps, showing up everywhere from seat cushions to window treatments. You'll also find patterns a home loom could create: checks, stripes, and plaids.

When choosing accessories to create the American country look, search flea markets, antique shops, and craft shows as well as conventional stores for handmade pieces—or at least pieces that look handmade. This style welcomes just about any piece that reflects a lifestyle that's close to the land: whimsical animals, wildflower-motif stencils, and interesting old farm and kitchen implements. All-American favorites are baskets, patchwork quilts, rag rugs, muslin curtains, hand-thrown pottery, creamware, and hand-carved toys.

In kitchen cabinets, everything from clean-lined Shaker to raised-panel traditional works well, in woods that range from elegantly grained maple to rustic, coarse-grained oak and pine. For a look that says this kitchen was assembled over time, don't be afraid to use open display shelving and cabinets in a mix of glass and solid doors, or even mix woodtone and painted cupboards together. As far as kitchen dining goes, you can't beat the classic farm table! It's perfect for impromptu crafts and helping with homework, too. Pair it with comb-backed, Windsor, ladder-backed, and other traditional chairs. And don't forget the kitchen rocker: the piece that best expresses the comfort of home and family, American country style.

High, Wide, and Handsome

IF YOU LOVE the sense of freedom you get from today's vaulted ceilings and light-filled windows, but you also love the warmth and tactile appeal of American country style, you can have both. This expansive kitchen proves it. Two-story-high walls of bleached knotty pine stay human-scaled with a soffit-height shelf showing off a giant American flag and antique decoys just above the traditional, divided-lite windows. (Modern picture windows would give a completely different effect.) The traditional wood cabinets below are echoed in the upper cabinets with punched-tin inserts. The speckled granite countertop on the island is timeless yet exciting, and the snug walkway between the L-shape work area and the island gives a sense of coziness. The whole effect is fresh yet friendly; the best of old and new.

Opposite: *Ample work space is right at hand's reach in this kitchen that boasts not only lots of counter surface but a large island, too. Like the best of islands, this one is great-looking and low-maintenance. It has room for two or more in casual dining as well as enough space to roll out a pie or lay out a casual buffet.*

A circle of friends can enjoy the view comfortably at this wonderful round table, lightly scaled in glass instead of the expected wood. Captain's chairs curve nicely around and give everyone, not just the hosts, the comfort of armrests. In this sparkling space, the slightly whimsical duck decoys look fresh again.

Spacious and Sensible

Hearty farmhouse style can be spacious and bright, as shown in this kitchen, with its white-painted walls and unobstructed windows along with up-to-the-minute stainless-steel appliances. The rest of the room is pure country at its most practical. Despite the open atmosphere, the kitchen is packed with storage. Cabinet units feature all the niches and shelving you'd ever need, and a massive island includes drawers and cupboards aplenty. Furthering the rustic mood of the knotty-pine upper cabinets, distressed-finished lower cabinets and chairs help create the authentic look, as if the kitchen were assembled from different wood pieces brought home over time. A kitchen like this makes a handsome showcase for antiques, kitchenware, and other interesting collectibles, including a sizable array of—what else?—cookbooks.

Above: *One roomy work island includes extra cooktop burners and a second sink, as well as enough counterspace to handle food preparation and serving. The butcher-block top and dark, distressed-wood cabinets are a dramatic contrast that works. Discreet wood knobs add a typically Shaker-style touch.*

Right: *This built-in combination of a desk and various storage pieces provides an extraordinarily useful, spacious home office right in the kitchen. A roomy, Shaker-style writing desk, bookcases, and cubbyhole storage above complete the setup.*

Opposite: *Dark woods lend a rustic look, but they don't close in this kitchen. The secret: white walls and ceiling; a wide, unshuttered window; light-reflecting stainless steel on the fridge and range hood; and plenty of unobtrusive ceiling spotlights.* **Designer: Kitchens by Deane.**

BAKER'S PRIDE
GATOR
MEAT

HANDSOME DARK-STAINED traditional cabinets and plain white walls create a country setting infused with dignity and warmth. Rustic baskets and a charming antique-style spice cabinet are perfect accents to this kitchen, as are the Windsor-backed chairs, striped rag rug, weathered cupboard, and vintage-style tin chandelier in the adjoining dining room. Keeping the look clean and simple helps the homeowner blend genuine antiques, like the dining room cupboard and table, with new but traditionally styled cabinets in the kitchen. The island houses the cooktop and provides easy access to the paneled side-by-side fridge nearby. Completing the work triangle is a sink under the double casement windows. A dark wood chair rail helps bring the white walls into the setting—just one of many subtle design touches that makes this space such a soothing, timeless place to be.

Left: *Dark cabinets and white walls make for a dramatic contrast, but tawny, wide-planked oak floors and mottled taupe granite countertops exert a mellowing influence. The mix of dark and midtone woods continues in the adjacent dining room, where an antique cupboard keeps company with the traditional-style scheme.*

Right: *A spacious, angled kitchen island with an inset cooktop offers up-to-date convenience in traditional American country style. Dark-stained cabinets with raised-panel doors and simple, matching wood knobs are topped with warm-toned granite counters.*

Colored With Charm

AMERICAN COUNTRY is chic these days, especially in a kitchen as artfully colored as this one. Classic icons, like the ladder-backed stools and rag rugs, carry the farmhouse-style message, and a jolt of fresh, brilliant color gives the whole room a wake-up call. Soothing expanses of naturally finished, traditional-style wood cabinets and flooring provide a feeling of spaciousness; a cheerful mix of patterns perks up the ceramic-tile backsplash and ruffled window valance. Vivid bits of handcrafted folk art displayed on counters and in glass-front cabinets add a richly inventive air. With all this artfulness, performance is still top priority: Bright, white appliances, including a spacious, side-by-side fridge with in-door water dispenser, deliver the goods in style. Overall, the color scheme of cobalt-blue, hunter-green, yellow, and white with warm wood tones is timeless yet lively. When color replaces clutter, the result is delicious.

Above: *Traditional glass-front, cathedral-arch cupboards with white ceramic knobs are sedate, but the brilliant mosaic folk art is anything but. This hunter-green, board-and-batten niche makes a perfect background for brightly colored art.* **Right:** *Black faux granite surfacing material is handsome enough on its own, but with the addition of inset green, blue, and yellow ceramic tiles, the effect is dazzling. It's practical, too: Ceramic tile makes a safe landing spot for hot dishes from the adjacent stove.*

Opposite: *Ladder-backed stools with rush seats bring an authentic, American country style to today's convenient island seating. The mellow country mood is echoed in natural-finish wood floors and cabinets, butcher-block island top, rag rugs, and classic Windsor dining chairs.*

COFFEE
RICE
TEA
FLOUR
OIL
PICKLES
NEWARK, N.J

WARM, RUSTIC, and hardworking, these kitchens take cooking very seriously. In one, the stove is a massive, commercial-style marvel that offers ovens and cooktops aplenty for rustling up a feast. In the other, the stove is a vintage charmer that provides ample cooking space and ovens, plus a heaping helping of nostalgia. In both, the color scheme—white, mustard, red, and cobalt-blue with wood—is a classic country favorite that has stood the test of time. In one kitchen, blue and white tiles set on an angle create an appealing border on the range hood and around the perimeter of the island's white ceramic-tile top. In the other, a small farm table with a white top doubles as an island. Everywhere, antique stoneware, ironware, and cooking bowls add to the rustic, hospitable atmosphere of a country past. If you're a serious antique kitchenware collector as well as a serious cook, what could be more natural?

Opposite: *Open storage, a signature of American country style, is abundant in this nostalgic yet practical kitchen. The china hutch/buffet angled in the corner shows off antique platters and other dishes; the pot rack over the island and the hooks for pans above the commercial stove keep cookware within reach.* ***Range: Wolf.***

Below: *An eat-in kitchen is one of the most popular aspects of country style, and this one is a classic. The ingredients are simple: a friendly round table and golden oak chairs, just steps away from the vintage stove. A classic farm table in the background is an ideal spot to stage dishes or land a hot pan.*

A Gift to Be Simple

ORDERLY BUT NOT COLD, this kitchen owes much to the clean, simple style of the Shakers, an early American religious sect of people whose motto was "cleanliness is next to godliness." Today's time-pressed homeowners still value a clean kitchen, and this uncluttered style makes it (relatively) easy to keep things in order. What's basic to Shaker style: beautifully crafted cabinets with the simplest hardware or none at all and plain walls, floors, and counters. Another important Shaker signature: rows of hooks or pegs for hanging cookware, baskets, and even chairs when they're not in use. Because these functional items are well-crafted, they engage the eye like artwork hanging on the wall. Hand-stitched quilts large and small, in surprisingly modern color combinations like red, black, and white, add more decorating punch.

Above: *Collectible handcrafts are abundant but out of the way of daily life in this practical eating nook under a window. A glass-front cabinet is filled with rare yellowware and other Early American finds that can be enjoyed from both the kitchen and the adjacent family room. The soffit-height shelf spanning the room affords even more space for showing off vintage treasures.*

Left: *A freestanding cupboard is part of an important decorating trend toward less-structured kitchen furniture. This snug little example in soft blue milkpaint houses jars of dry goods, but it would work just as well for homemade preserves or any attractive items. A classically Shaker row of wall pegs shows off charming collectibles of many kinds.*

Handsome recessed-panel cabinets attract attention when the overall scheme is simple. Plain white laminate countertops do the job without adding visual clutter—the better to show off vintage spice boxes and racks. Hanging baskets are classic Shaker.

PEACHES
BLUEBERRYS
EGGS
BREAD
Phenix

Another Roadside Attraction

BUOYANT RED-AND-WHITE CHECKS express the fresh spirit of a farmhouse better than almost any other color combination or print. This kitchen gets every touch right, from the white cabinetry with simple iron hardware to the sturdy farm table with an authentic tinware candelabra above. The impromptu pot rack made of suspended pipe holds a full complement of cooking pots; in this case, the vintage white enamel pots with red handles so familiar in the 1930s and '40s. The full-length glass doors opening onto a white picket-fenced deck are a departure from the past that makes sense for today. The stenciled produce stand signs, misspellings and all, are a charming touch that draws the eye upward to the handsome, narrow-board ceiling. The feeling is frisky but not too cute; just right for a breezy, welcoming kitchen.

Left: *A sturdy farm table is a welcome sight, especially when paired with traditional bow-backed chairs. The island and countertops provide ample work space, but it's nice to have the table as an extra staging surface when needed. Careful editing of the colors used in accessories throughout the room keeps the look consistent, not cluttered.*

Right: *Red-and-white checked curtains and ruffled valance lend a cheerful picnic feeling to this lighthearted kitchen. The collection of mini-birdhouses brings even more nature home. The practical double sink in stainless steel reflects the cool metallic sheen of the pierced-tin hanging lamp.*

A Rich Custom Blend

WARM COLORS and romantic accessories transport this homeowner to a sunny climate and give the country kitchen a slightly exotic accent. Kitchens like this are proof that you don't have to play by the rules even with a tried-and-true style like American country, as long as you keep your color scheme a bit disciplined and your accessories in the same mood throughout. The handsome combination of painted and naturally finished wood cabinets creates depth and the look of a freestanding kitchen that has evolved over time. The innovations continue with handsome plaid fabric squares tossed casually over curtain rods to create one-of-a-kind valances. The dining nook is an engaging blend of eras and styles: A colorful, airy printed fabric adorns the banquette seating, traditional sheaf-of-wheat chairs provide open seating, and a Tiffany-style lamp hangs overhead. Unique windowpane-inspired wall hangings enclose a variety of whimsical images. Who says tradition can't be individualistic?

Above: *Two-toned cabinets with turned-leg details below and a bullnose pediment above suggest freestanding furniture without sacrificing the convenience of built-ins. Open shelving shows off yellowware and other collectibles; a row of cubbyhole-size drawers hides incidentals while adding visual interest.*

Right: *A romantic dining nook is the sum of many whimsical elements, from the fabric-covered banquette to the stained-glass lamp and unique wall hangings. Just a few touches—woven striped placemats, dried flowers, baskets, and candles—create a relaxing environment.*

Eggplant and spice colors give a different twist to casually draped window valance fabric and tie in nicely with the two tones of wood cabinetry. Keeping everything cool, the modern white gooseneck faucet and white microwave and countertops add a jolt of freshness. Brass and copper molds are classically elegant, while delightful birdhouses give a slightly rustic air. **Designer: Sandra E. Arabia.**

Butter-Nut BREAD

FOR PEOPLE who can't get enough of the lustrous beauty of naturally finished wood, this kitchen offers a wealth of traditional charm. Start with the cabinets: an interesting mix of wood and glass doors to hide or show off contents as you like, embellished with simple, yet elegant, brass hardware. Add a nicely finished wood strip floor, polished to show off the grain. Bring in ladder-backed chairs with gracefully curved tops, and add a generously scaled, friendly round table. Keep the ceiling, backsplash, and counters neutral to let the wood play the starring role, but, to avoid monotony, add the spark of an all-time-favorite color combination: red, white, and blue. In this restful setting, vintage collectibles can really shine. The cheerful color scheme is nicely balanced—just like the room itself.

Below: *One wonderful quilt makes a dramatic tablecloth. It's a fun way to show off your own creative handiwork or a great antique-shop find. Plump seat cushions in the same blue as the quilt add more softness and color and also keep the abundance of wood from becoming overwhelming.*

Opposite: *This is the type of country kitchen that's easily achievable and right for almost any traditional home. A wood floor and cabinets, all finished in honeyed hues, and a window with just a simple valance work together to create a soothing background for an array of collectibles in slightly muted primary colors.* ***Designer: Helen Norman, Broad Street Antiques and Collectibles.***

Collectible canisters and boxes from long-gone general stores add a nostalgic note to this kitchen's decorative accessories. A grapevine wreath, blue spatterware vase, and row of diminutive birdhouses are standard American country icons that fit right in here.

A LOG CABIN KITCHEN is as cozy as can be, enriched with delightful details to be uncovered at every turn. Dark wood cabinets blend into the soundly chinked wood walls, broken only by unpretentious white laminate countertops. A small round table made of old planked wood seats four on equally old (or old-looking) dining chairs, none matching. This nicely sized table also doubles as extra work space. A microwave is cunningly hidden behind an old-time creamery's sign, and overhead, an array of big baskets and pierced-tin pendant lights share the ceiling space. In the larger dining area, a whitewashed wall brings in more light, while a handsome antique china cupboard takes the spotlight, its doors flung wide to show off a fine collection of antique ceramics in tawny tones. This is one kitchen where impromptu bouquets of wildflowers or autumn leaves are perfectly at home.

Opposite: *Crowded but comfortable, this kitchen nestles discreet, black-glass-front appliances between dark wood cabinets. The microwave? It's behind the yellow creamery sign. The round table is just the right size for a few to share a bite or labor over a homework project. A row of cone-shaped, pierced-tin downlights offer ample task lighting.* ***Designer: Gloria Hilderbrand, Country Store of Seven Springs.***

Left: *A showcase cupboard filled with antique ceramics is the focal point of this dining area. A whitewashed wall relieves the darkness of the planked wood walls and overhead beams and makes the most of reflected sunlight. Children's chairs in jewel tones add a bright touch.*

FRESH EGGS FOR SALE
Purina Chows
BROCK
CHOCOLATE COVERED
HERSHEY'S
NEW ENGLAND
Ask For
T.C.
TORRINGTON CREAMERY
Ice Cream at its Best
DAVIS
SATISFACTION GUARANTEED
Dwinell-Wright Company
Boston Coffees
PURE LARD

Pioneer Simplicity

ONE AMERICAN COUNTRY STYLE that works as well in a small kitchen as in a large one is Shaker. Its clean, pared-down look is both visually uncluttered and practical—just what you'd expect from a style with its origins in a religion that held cleanliness next to godliness. This kitchen doesn't lack for square footage, but the simplicity of Shaker style still shines through. On the ceiling, old recycled beams contribute a rustic look, while floorboards are finished smoothly for easy care. A commercial-style black stove sits next to one small open cabinet that functions as a work surface, and a black Shaker-style table looks surprisingly spiffy with a whitewashed top and coordinating white-painted chairs. Yellowware bowls, a wall-hung spice rack, and a striped rag rug are Early American icons that seal the look.

Right: *To make the most of the space you have, adopt a Shaker solution: a variety of small wooden hanging shelves and cupboards that keep the floor clear. Round wooden baskets, like the graduated-size stack near the door, are among the most collectible Shaker antiques. If those are out of reach, look for square fruit boxes like those on the table.*

Opposite: *Shaker-style chairs with woven rattan seats get a fresh look with white paint, as does the top of the black-painted Shaker table.*

Americana collectibles from every era are hotter than ever, and the kitchen is a natural place to show them off. In this kitchen, vintage baskets, copper cooking molds, wooden rolling pins, and related cookware celebrate old-time ingenuity. To keep these many items from creating a disorderly look, organization is key: Grouping like items together creates a cohesive, less-cluttered appearance. To further the warmhearted, nostalgic look, antique (and antique-looking) appliances and accessories are used wherever possible. But this room is faithful to the spirit of American country in a way that goes beyond collectibles. A kitchen big enough to serve as a gathering place for family and friends is a must, and this room has all the space needed to make casual hospitality a snap.

Above: *An antique-style stove and a fine old porcelain-on-cast-iron sink are unique focal points in the work area. Nearby, a vintage-style kitchen island that looks like a great antique takes a practical, modern turn with a granite top.*

Opposite: *Copper and baskets, two of the most popular Americana collectibles, shine in this kitchen. There's ample space for both on overhead beam hooks that keep treasures in sight but out of the way. There's plenty of room for folk art, vintage tin pieces, and a great collection of old rolling pins, too.*

Right: *An eat-in kitchen is basic to American country style, and this one has plenty of room for a table that seats six without crowding the space. A handsome oak floor is made even more dramatic with large, painted diamonds.*

COFFEE
AND SPICES

IF YOU LIKE a kitchen with a bit more frivolity and romance than the staid Shaker style typically allows, borrow a few 19th-century European touches, as Americans have always done. This country kitchen is so pretty and full of fun, it looks ready for an old-fashioned garden party all the time. The first thing you notice is the sparkling white, glass-front cabinets and the striking ceramic tile countertops in cobalt-blue-and-white checkerboard. Against this crisp, eye-catching background, cheerful yellow wall-coverings and window valences in a classic French provincial print bring in the sunshine. Timeless frosted-glass hanging lamps are sparked with brass for added sparkle, day or night. The homeowner's porcelain, glass, and other vintage collectibles, most of them colorfully patterned, add to the genial mix. The casual dining table is snuggled right up to the work area for friendly kibitzing with the cook. When the table's not set, it offers extra space for food prep or an informal buffet.

Fruits and flowers on a custom-designed stove backsplash give the dynamic duo of cobalt-blue and white tiles a special focus. An array of classic copper cooking tools and a hanging wall rack for spices and oils add more country flavor.

Left: *A little romance in the form of French provincial wallcoverings and ruffled valances; pretty, frosted hanging lamps; and a flower basket motif on the ceramic tile backsplash give this American country kitchen a fresh accent. The blue, white, and yellow color scheme, punctuated with rooster-comb red, is a never-fail recipe for a cheerful space.*

Left: *A clutch of collectibles, including porcelain poultry, books, and small ceramic boxes in paintbox colors, adds to the cheery ambience of this kitchen. Small free-standing furniture pieces, like this curvy bookcase and old icebox, add warmth and character. Overhead, there's more country charm in a row of copper molds and a hanging rack for colanders and baskets.*

Commercial Chic

ARE YOU an ambitious cook, a frequent entertainer, or just a fan of great restaurants? Commercial chic style brings high-performance, restaurant-quality appliances into your home, along with the pizzazz they convey to their settings. You'll want to do plenty of research to find just the right commercial-grade appliances that will work for you, because innovations are happening all the time. In general, you'll be in the market for the most practical, high-powered products available, made for heavy use and for feeding more than the average number of diners. Your commercial chic kitchen will probably include some or all of these performing greats: stoves with six burners instead of the usual four, plus an optional stovetop grill unit; huge, side-by-side stainless-steel refrigerator/freezers; double wall ovens; specialized, stainless-steel sinks; and so on.

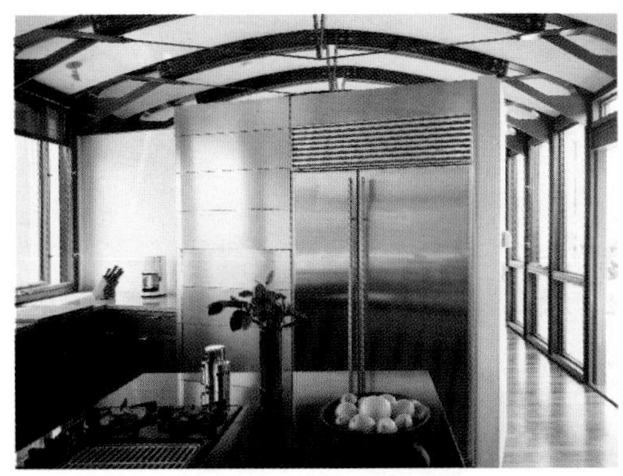

Whatever appliances you decide on, you'll no doubt want to surround them with high-quality materials that stand up to heavy use, just as bona fide commercial kitchens do. For your home kitchen, however, "durable" doesn't need to mean "institutional." So specify durable granite or solid-surface countertops, some with butcher-block cutting surfaces. Polished granite repels spills better than unpolished, and it adds light-catching sparkle to the space, while solid-surface countertops can be scoured clean easily, even of minor burns and stains. Choose solid hardwood or metal cabinetry (either brushed stainless steel or commercially painted with appliance-grade paint) with easy-to-use door and drawer pulls. Go for glossy ceramic wall tiles or high-gloss paint in luscious colors, from eggplant to buttercream—they're an exciting contrast to metallic tones or black. Commercial kitchens emphasize safety (think multiple cooks, all moving quickly!) so be sure to specify no-slip ceramic, natural-stone, or even commercial rubber floor tiles. And don't forget counter-height stools for kibitzing guests, because your commercial chic kitchen is definitely user-friendly.

Steamship Sleek

A commercial-style, stainless-steel refrigerator embedded in a short wall attains a sculptural look. The drop-in gas cooktop with a built-in grill hardly disturbs the mirror-like calm of the polished, black granite counter.

SLEEK AND SHINING, this commercial-style kitchen makes the best use of space while providing a dramatic, exciting environment to work in and enjoy, day and night. Great expanses of shining stainless steel and polished granite make for slick, no-nonsense surfaces that convey one of the most important kitchen qualities: cleanliness. The latest appliances weigh in with workhorse strength and showhouse appeal. Lighting is unobtrusive, with the effect, not the source, most important. Windows play an important role in maximizing the light captured by shiny kitchen surfaces. When all is said and done, a kitchen designed with commercial chic like this serves up professionalism, performance, and just plain good looks. It's a sophisticated look especially at home in urbane environments—perhaps like yours.

At first glance, this kitchen dazzles with its expanses of shiny surfaces—polished granite, stainless steel, and clear glass. What's even more intriguing, however, is the exciting strength of the design, evidenced in the wall of appliances and the wood-and-steel ceiling struts.

Left: *Steel-sparked ivory and pink create a luxurious kitchen. An off-white island, held up at the counter end with a stainless column, has plenty of room for coffee shop stools. The diamond-bordered floor defines the work corridors from the center of the room. A commercial-type refrigerator/ freezer and stove and range hood, all in stainless steel, blend sleekly into the cabinet area.*

Posh in Platinum and Pink

THE FIRST THING you notice about this kitchen is its extraordinary color scheme: silvery steel, ivory, and blush, the color of a soft rosé wine or perhaps a vintage cocktail. It's not the usual color scheme for a kitchen, but it's perfect for this splendid art deco room. Subtle pink-toned marble floors are enlivened with a diamond-motif border. The pretty look is repeated on the backsplash and makes an interesting counterpoint to the expanses of stainless-steel cabinetry around it. Seating is a lighthearted mix of ivory deco-slatted chairs, a comfortable window banquette, and plump coffee shop stools with pale blush fabric cushions. Metals are a combination of shiny stainless and brushed steel (now often called "nickel finish") that has an almost pewterlike, soft luster. The overall effect is one of luxury, refinement, and up-to-the-minute chic that's urbane, gracious, and somehow timeless.

Left: *Dining style is easy with this ivory oval table, art deco–inspired chairs, and cushioned banquette under the window. To the right of the dining area, a sound system and home office are built in.*

Free-Form and Fabulous

Interesting shapes on layered planes make this beguiling little snack station aesthetically appealing and extremely useful. Thick glass, wood, and metal elements are also easy to keep clean.

THERE'S NOTHING ORDINARY about this kitchen, which looks playful but has every element engineered flawlessly. On one side of the oversize range, a white counter, jigsawed in a giant French curve, embraces the work area. On the other side, a modern wood-and-stainless countertop echoes the curve, as does an ingenious stainless, glass, and wood snack counter. In the back of the room, a cheerful red C-curve banquette provides seating for larger groups. Above the stove, a pair of sculpturally appealing cabinets follows the line of the minimalist glass range hood. It's a great way to provide lots of conventional cooking-area storage—without a conventional look. This kitchen is proof that super-modern doesn't have to mean minimalist or severe. This kind of creative, highly intelligent design defies expectations but never loses sight of the performance needs a kitchen has to meet. It's a design that puts the "fun" back in functional.

Right: *A high-tech stove takes the conventional cooktop, oven, and range hood combo to a whole new level of visual drama and performance. The stainless-steel design incorporates its own countertop surfaces on each side of the cooktop as well as in the cabinetry below, which lets the range be used on a wall by itself.*

Right: *A lipstick-red banquette and judicious use of pale wood balances the extreme, metallic modernity of the overall scheme. The curves found in the counters, tables, and even in the high-tech appliances also soften the strong, metal-dominated setting.*

Low-Slung Elegance

A MODERN CLASSIC inspired by Frank Lloyd Wright and other stellar postwar architects, this kitchen is all restful horizontal lines that create a very different kind of elegance than what is found in vertically oriented traditional styles. A long, shallow window runs the length of one wall, providing an intimate view of the gardens outside. The sink, located on this wall, features ample counterspace on either side. A separate cooktop and oven are staggered rather than stacked along the adjacent wall to allow two cooks to work out of each other's way. For visual balance and convenience, a dark glass-fronted microwave is situated overhead on the same wall. Generous expanses of wood, from the exposed overhead beams to the strip flooring, are echoed in the wood cabinets that also feature a horizontal grain.

Left: *Horizontal lines create a harmonious rhythm that's the hallmark of excellent architecture. In this case, the look is carried out in the strong overhead beams, windowsill, countertops, and even the grain of the cabinets. Naturally, the wood floor was laid on the same axis so that the grain of the flooring runs parallel to the rest of the room's lines.*

Right: *Stark simplicity imparts a sense of calm and strength in this kitchen's design. The dark masses of the conventional oven and microwave are balanced by the pale expanses of drawers and base cabinets. Even the cabinet hardware is in sync: unadorned, narrow horizontal wood strips. In a minimalist aesthetic like this one, the details are few, and every one counts.*

A Shipshape Solution

THERE'S A PLACE for everything in this neatly conceived kitchen that makes good use of corners and angles. Clean expanses of wood are punctuated by the dazzle of stainless steel and chrome, not clutter. Appliances, including a double oven, microwave, dishwasher, fridge, and more are all built in, as is the TV. Warm-toned wood cabinets in modern style are balanced by expanses of mottled granite counters and a stainless-steel commercial-style range and backsplash. Generously scaled, curved stainless-steel door and drawer pulls are small details that pack a lot of design punch. Lights inset in the ceiling provide ample task and ambient lighting; strategically placed lights beneath the upper cabinets add dramatic accents. Everything the semiprofessional chef and a bevy of "assistants" might need is here, all wrapped up in one handsome design solution.

Left: *A brushed stainless range hood and wall panel with built-in hanging utensil rack help the commercial-style range become a pleasing focal point. On the right, a modern wall rack of spices, dramatically down-lit, is both practical and colorful.*

Right: *This practical kitchen island houses the sink, the dishwasher, plenty of prep space, and room for a pair of casual diners. The clean design lets eye-catching cooking equipment, like the stainless-steel scale, take center stage.* **Designer: Madison Design.**

Contemporary

A CONTEMPORARY KITCHEN is like a breath of fresh air—it's cool and comfortable, and it can be as casual or as elegant as you please. At home in most settings, classic contemporary is softer than modern, cleaner than traditional, and easy to live with. One of the most versatile contemporary looks is often identified "California style," as originated by the late designer Michael Taylor. This refreshing look translates into spacious, sensually casual white rooms that use pastels (tropical or pale) and every tone of white-on-white, from warm ivory to cool oyster-shell gray. Scandinavian contemporary, a cheerful look that works well in kitchens as well as in kids' rooms, pairs whites with one or more bright primary colors. Art deco, an urbane contemporary style, sparks pale neutrals with black and metallic tones. The Miami variant adds aqua and coral; for New York-to-Paris panache, add ice-blue and mauve.

Whatever contemporary style suits you, keep the look streamlined and fuss-free. Choose built-in cabinets and small dining groups that make clever use of every square inch, and add sparkle with chrome banding, edges, and hardware. If you want a metallic look that disguises wear, choose a brushed- or nickel-finish stainless steel with a soft patina. The contemporary look revels in all the modern appliances and inventions, so you don't need to hide them unless you want to. Open floor plans, view-embracing windows, abstract prints, adventurous color combinations, and interesting textures are all part of the freedom-loving contemporary look. It's a natural for the kitchen, where clean lines mean easy cleanup. Go for the smooth sweep of marble, granite, solid-surface, or laminate counters. Choose frameless cabinets with flat doors and finger-grooves instead of pulls. Opt for brass, glass, and brushed- or stainless-steel dining tables paired with leather or vinyl-seated chairs. These are all the latest conveniences that give contemporary kitchens all the comforts of home.

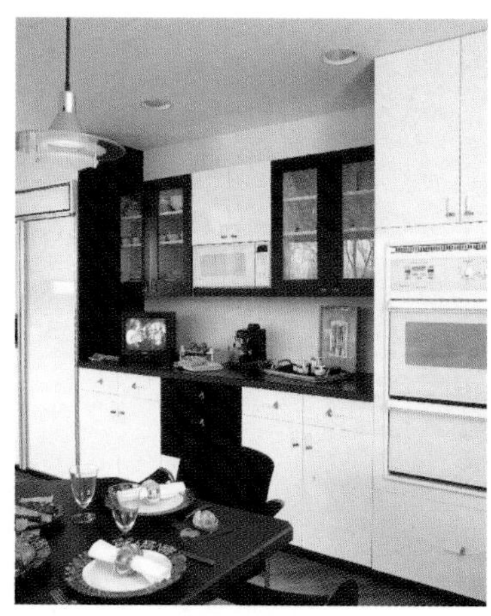

Throw Nature a Curve

Spectacular vistas of desert and mountains front the informal dining area. Against this kind of competition, the homeowners wisely chose a small, witty echo of the view outside: a substantial but very simple marble block that holds a slender square of glass for informal dining. In more ordinary environments, this table and the marble and stainless-steel kitchen would afford a pretty spectacular view on their own.

THE VIEWS inside this cutting-edge kitchen are almost as stunning as those of the awesome mountains and desert outside. The shell is a subtle blend of cool white walls and floor and warm ivory cabinets—an unusual combination that creates a sense of depth. Beautiful, swirl-patterned marble creates a handsome counter and backsplash, but the real tour de force is the silvery half-round island, a sculptural marvel that evokes the space-age spirit of freedom. The sink, with its sculpted faucet, is housed in the island, while the cooktops are located on one wall and the wall ovens on the other. The whole effect is one of remarkable engineering and deceptive simplicity born of great expertise and applied with care and creativity. Not everyone is up for such a sophisticated kitchen, but for those who are, the reward is a one-of-a-kind space where, in the best contemporary style, form follows function—beautifully.

Right: *The space-age island is a stunning example of functional design. In one pleasing, semicircular mass, it houses open shelving, closed-drawer storage, a sink, warming drawers, and more. The black-glass wall oven stands alone; a run of countertop with a luxurious marble backsplash abuts the cooktop under the window. Marble and stainless steel make great companions in a kitchen like this.*

A Feast for the Eyes

Above: *A microwave stationed between the fridge and the sink makes short work of preparing snacks and quick meals. The under-counter location is practical for the disabled as well as for children who are old enough to fix their own goodies.*

THIS REMARKABLE KITCHEN is proof that color is always the most compelling design element. To get the look, these homeowners started with a pristine white ceiling and floor, the better to contrast with color. Glossy cabinets in a great shade of blue-green were paired with pure white countertops, sink, faucets, and fridge. The dishwasher has a teal front panel to match the cabinets, and the tour de force—the commercial-style range—is also in matching teal. A lively mix of blues, accented by green and cheerful buttercream-yellow ceramic tiles, creates an appealing backsplash. On the practical side, the under-counter microwave is located next to the fridge for fast snack preparation, and a skylight above the sink amplifies the light from the window. It's contemporary at its most playful, creative best.

Left: *Paintbox tiles on the backsplash combine blues, green, and yellow in a cheerful color scheme. The curved counter provides handicapped access during food preparation or any time.*

Opposite: *Deep blue-green on the cabinets and commercial-style stove give this kitchen a unique look. Cut with lots of white, the result is fresh and cool. A casual dining table with banquette seating is just steps away.*

Blond Sparked With Black

Sophisticated style has an added flash of elegance, thanks to decorative wood mullions on the lighted glass display cabinets. Gleaming black counters and a glass peninsula table add further sparkle. Pale wood strip flooring continues the mellow, expansive look of the handsome wood cabinets. ***Designer: Bruce Colucci, CKD, Le Gourmet Kitchen.***

Soothing expanses of pale wood accented with shiny black create a sophisticated kitchen scheme. The kitchen with the corner-wrapping window features not one, but two stainless-steel stoves with matching stainless range hoods and a built-in warming drawer. It's an ideal space for a pair of cabinet drawers accented with the modern signature of routed finger pulls instead of conventional knobs or handles. The kitchen with the glass peninsula set for two has a side-by-side refrigerator with wood panels that match the rest of the elegant cabinetry. This kitchen also features the postmodern touch of fan-shaped window mullions in the upper, lighted cabinets. In addition to pale wood cabinets and black countertops, these kitchens share the use of recessed ceiling lighting that's unobtrusive but shoots a lot of light into the work area. That's a design solution that's purely contemporary.

Cool and flooded with light, this kitchen makes the most of modern window technology to wrap the view and create an unbeatable focal point above the corner sink. At each end of the adjacent cabinet runs, a gleaming stainless-steel stove and range hood provide enough cooking space for a crew and, with the sink, create overlapping work triangles.
Designer: Ultimate Kitchens.

Bentwood chairs in shiny black wood follow the curves of the countertop; seats, like the counter itself, are banded in racing-stripe red. Even the smoked-glass dining table has rounded corners. It's a nice touch that softens the look and is safer than sharp corners, too. ***Designer: Janine Jordan, CKD, IIDA, IDS; JJ Interiors. Countertops: DuPont Corian.***

Gray Flashed in Red

COOL GRAY, one of the most livable neutrals, is a sophisticated choice for any modern setting. With a flashy injection of bright red, the light and midtone grays in this kitchen really take off. (A similar effect could be achieved with another color as long as it's bright and on the warm side—chrome-yellow or lime-green, perhaps.) Everything that can be built in is, including the white microwave oven and cooktop set into the countertop. (Positioning the microwave away from the conventional cooktop and ovens creates a second prep space for warming up foods without disrupting the main work triangle.) Smoked-glass cupboard doors above the snack counter enclose glassware; solid-door cupboards, laminated in pale gray, follow the countertop's curves. The overall effect is a fun, contemporary city look, wherever it may be.

Right: *A racy red range hood is the obvious focal point of this part of the kitchen. Everything else, except for a fun red faucet and the red banding along the countertop edge, is in soothing shades of gray. Where a black-and-white checkerboard tile floor might be too jarring in a small space, this pale and dark gray pattern provides just enough visual interest. Small gray ceramic tiles make up the easy-care backsplash.* ***Flooring: American Olean. Faucet: Delta.***

Above: *Smoked glass tops the dining table, in keeping with the gray tones of the room. Black, white, gray, and red tabletop items carry the theme further with ease. The subtle touches of red, as well as the theme-and-variation of black, white, and gray tones, make this room easy on the eyes.* ***Cabinets: Rutt.***

Set in Stone

White cabinetry expands the space in this long, relatively narrow corridor that includes both a bar-type sink and the kitchen's main sink. The second sink is ideal for entertaining. Plain, meticulously crafted cabinets showcase decorative accessories. ***Refrigerator: KitchenAid.***

MATTE-FINISHED gray tile with the look of stone creates an architecturally interesting focal point in a large-scaled kitchen. The overall design is textbook-savvy: For safety's sake, the cooktop inset into the countertop is stepped down a few inches. The fridge, cooktop, and sink are steps apart in a classic work triangle, with the dishwasher adjoining the sink. On the other side of the fridge, a second sink and extra storage create another convenient work area. Custom cabinetry opposite this second sink is a stunning showcase for the homeowners' fine blue-and-white glass and porcelain collections. White walls and cabinets create a perfect background for the soothing gray floor and countertops. The emphasis here is on quiet performance, not flash.

Right: *Clean, simple lines, rather than color, set the tone of this kitchen. Textured gray tile makes a subtly interesting countertop with plenty of space for informal dining as well as for the drop-in cooktop. Over the sink, a pleasing, triple casement window provides ample natural light.* ***Designer: Kitchens & Baths by Louise Gilmartin. Cabinets: Heritage Custom Kitchens; cooktop: Thermador; dishwasher: Miele.***

arc de triomphe

Playing the Angles

Sharp contrasts like this black-and-white scheme make for a dramatic look, but when you add sharp angles to the mix, the visual excitement really heats up. This modern kitchen adds even more drama by varying the heights of the countertops. The result is a sculptural, no-frills look that's slick but never monotonous. White base cabinets are topped with black countertops, creating a visual rhythm with an alternating array of white and black cabinets above. A wall of cabinets housing the microwave and generous storage is flanked by a side-by-side fridge and wall oven. While most of the lighting is provided by unobtrusive recessed task light fixtures, a gleaming, modern hanging lamp, suspended over the table, performs the timeless function of a chandelier. Everything is carefully planned and executed; one might say these homeowners got it all down in black and white.

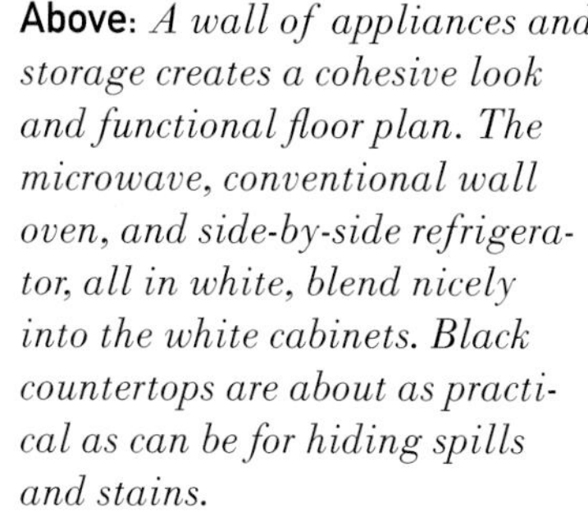

Above: *A wall of appliances and storage creates a cohesive look and functional floor plan. The microwave, conventional wall oven, and side-by-side refrigerator, all in white, blend nicely into the white cabinets. Black countertops are about as practical as can be for hiding spills and stains.*

Left: *Angled for convenience and style, this L-shape cabinet configuration defines both the work space and the dining space. Instead of the predictable black-and-white tiled flooring you might expect in a high-contrast scheme like this, the naturally finished wood flooring and window frames add an unexpected touch of warmth.*

Opposite: *The dining table adjoins a matching countertop, but placing it a few inches lower maximizes floor space while defining the eating area. It also makes informal service very convenient.*

Drama in Black and Gold

Below: *The gold triangle over the drop-in cooktop is an exciting focal point for this dramatic kitchen. The entire stove backsplash area is embellished with black-and-gold custom tiles. Jewel-like tiles throughout are made of steel, copper, and cracked glass as well as ceramic.* ***Designer: Gary White, CKD, CBD, CID, Kitchen & Bath Design.***

Golden wood cabinetry banded in black, wood floors that blend tawny tones from dark brown to blond, and custom black-and-gold tile accents make a contemporary statement that's warmly dramatic. A triangular motif is expressed in "the wedge"—a globe-studded, brushed-stainless light fixture suspended over the peninsula. This triangle is echoed in the textured-glass panels on the upper display cabinets. Pale gray striated marble countertops and gleaming charcoal-gray backsplash tiles provide a cooling transition and make the custom gold-and-black decorative tiles really stand out. With all this drama, the basics are not overlooked. An efficient work triangle with trash compactor and double sinks, plenty of perimeter cabinet storage and countertops, and a convenient dining peninsula make this space hardworking as well as handsome.

Right: *Light-and-dark drama is found throughout this kitchen, which has a festive air thanks in part to the sparkling play of light on highly polished kitchen surfaces and the homeowner's collection of art glass. Pendant lamps over the integrated table cast a fractured pattern on the ceiling.*

ONE OF THE most perennially appealing modern looks—pale wood punctuated with black accents—is used to good effect in this clean-lined kitchen. The kitchen owes a lot of its cool good looks to bird's-eye maple with a simple, natural stain. The stiles and rails are book-matched, an unusually meticulous treatment, so that the wood grain runs continuously down the side of a bank of drawers. Solid black granite countertops combined with black-lacquered ceiling moldings and toe kicks add definition between floor, ceiling, and cabinets while creating a snappy overall accent. The wood over the window and doors reflects the same panel detailing seen on the island cabinets. Soft sandstone tiles cover the backsplash area above each counter and surround the window. The overall look is subdued yet sophisticated.

Opposite: *The range, backsplash, shelf, and vent hood with two built-in heat lamps all sparkle in stainless steel. Other stainless-steel accents include the practical waste chute fitted through the island's granite countertop and the undermounted sink beneath the oversize bay window.* **Designer: Ben Kuypers. Range: Thermador; dishwasher: Bosch; faucet: Grohe.**

Above: *The microwave with trim kit is tucked into a corner for maximum efficiency and minimum fuss. Below it is a pantry with pullouts. The adjacent refrigerator in stainless steel coordinates with the range.* **Refrigerator: Sub-Zero.**

Below: *A neat little desk area is tucked beneath an attractive glass-door cabinet with interior lights to show off the homeowner's crystal. Next to the desk, a pantry cupboard is topped with a practical, 42-cubicle wine rack that acts as another design element.* **Manufacturer: T.L. Precision Cabinets.**

Visual Excitement

SHAPE AND TEXTURE reign in this eye-catching kitchen. One exciting focal point is the large wraparound snack island with silvery, pearlized granite top. Function and style combine handsomely in the island's raised glass snack bar and undermounted stainless-steel sink. One wall, visually enhanced by a natural rock section, houses the microwave, fridge, and double oven. Another offers a combination gas and electric cooktop with overhead vent and ample counterspace on both sides. The ventilation system is fully accessible behind curved, bird's-eye maple doors that match the curved cooktop cabinet and fridge panels. Overhead, a pine-paneled ceiling is bisected with gray painted beams and brightened with a skylight over the work area. Small suspended halogen lights are works of art that provide ample task lighting.

Opposite: *The double oven, fridge, microwave, and additional storage space are all built into one wall to maximize this kitchen's space. The adjacent fieldstone wall inspired the kitchen's color scheme.*

Left: *Chrome posts bolted to the top of the C-shape island's mica-flecked granite countertop hold a ¾-inch-thick glass eating bar that measures nine feet long. The marbleized fabric of the counter stools completes the exciting design theme.* ***Designer: Ben Kuypers. Manufacturer: T.L. Precision Cabinets.***

The two-tiered kitchen island houses the cooktop, a second sink, and lots of food prep space. A column light, suspended over the length of the work space, further emphasizes the kitchen's unique ceiling heights.
Designer: Lila Levinson, ASID, CKD, CID, Accent On Design.

A Sunny Perspective

THIS BRIGHT, open-air kitchen is clean and contemporary, yet very livable, thanks to its effortless connection with nature. First, it provides the most wonderful of garden views with lots of large windows and glass doors all around. White-painted walls and high ceilings add to the fresh, spacious feeling. The high ceilings are brought into balance with long, suspended lights that run the length of the work space. This kitchen is as efficient as it is attractive, thanks in large part to a spacious island and armoire-style cupboard, both providing maximum storage space. On the wall housing the double oven, microwave, and refrigerator, small appliances find a home on the counter and in an appliance garage hidden behind a tambour roll-top door. A suspended upper cabinet and base cabinet on one end help define the kitchen area.

Surrounding the main sink under the window, bright cobalt-blue tile countertops add a festive look; the blue color is carried out in other accent pieces throughout the kitchen.

Cool Formality

MODERN STYLE'S emphasis on function over decoration doesn't have to mean an absence of beauty. In this handsome kitchen, finely crafted cabinets with gently rounded corners and a large rounded island offer visual appeal with their sophisticated pale stain. A stove backsplash and black granite countertops are exciting touches; black toe kicks and moldings on each cabinet add a snappy accent. A simple pleated shade moderates the sunshine streaming in through the oversize window above the sink. An acoustical ceiling with large beams in a glossy white finish is an important attention-getter in its own right. The major focal point of the room, the island, holds a second sink, ample food preparation space, and an informal dining area. In a room this simple, every element, including the range hood and the pendant light over the island, adds to the sleek design statement.

Opposite: *Half-round stainless-steel posts embellish the curved maple panels on the handsome island while enhancing the kitchen's sparkling appliances and black granite countertops. The counter stools themselves are sculpturally intriguing, with an art deco–inspired rocket-shape design.* **Designer: Ben Kuypers.**

Left: *Maple cabinets, stained in a sophisticated opal tone and featuring flat panels with mitered frames, have a cool and elegant look. The cabinets' rounded edges complement the spacious island.* **Manufacturer: Merit Kitchens.**

Eclectic

Art collectors, world travelers, and sophisticated homeowners everywhere crave the wit and dignity of eclectic style. A deft blend of antique and modern, practical and inspirational, eclectic style takes the best from many eras and makes it your own. Eclectic style seems made for today's kitchens, where, of necessity, many modern elements are used, but old-fashioned hospitality and warmth are still desired. In this style, designer know-how really helps, because the principles of balance, traffic flow, and color coordination count most when the look isn't limited to a style or two.

Within these ground rules, have some fun. Pick your favorite design elements, and team them up. Try pairing the warmth of traditional, fine-hardwood cabinetry with the sparkle of modern lighting; a contemporary, brass-and-glass table with Shaker side chairs; a French country armoire with a run of solid-surface counters. To achieve balance, intersperse large pieces of different eras but the same approximate visual "weight" around the room:

For example, see how the mass of a modern stove in black enameled steel is balanced when flanked by traditional cabinets with wrought-iron pulls. Or choose another popular interpretation of eclectic for the kitchen: Embellish mostly modern large pieces (cabinets and appliances) with antique accessories that add texture, personality, and warmth. The contrast can be invigorating, and you may be surprised at how much a modern steel piece has in common with a simple Shaker implement that was equally functional in its day.

What works with everything: Asian art and textiles that celebrate nature in a stylized, timeless way; dhurrie rugs, their ancient styles as geometric as Cubist modern art; glass of every kind; rich, jewel-tone colors that are elegant and a bit exotic; shapes that are either pared way down or flawlessly crafted. Eclectic style says the journey's the thing, but you've definitely arrived.

Christian Dior

Amethyst Backdrop

HERE'S A KITCHEN fit for an artist or another fearlessly romantic individualist. Sure, it plays fast and loose with the rules about what's "proper," but it's loyal to the rules of great design: proportion, repetition, and balance. When launching a look this unusual, a healthy dose of confidence and a bit of design know-how really help. The effect is wild, but every bit of it is cleverly planned, and that's the essence of eclectic style success. In contrast to the luscious amethyst-colored walls, reeded white cabinets and white trim pop brightly. The purple tones are echoed in the backsplash and the checkerboard fabric on the small traditional chair. A pair of squared-off, Shaker-style counter stools and a nearby dining table bring in slightly golden wood tones. A traditionally curvaceous chandelier and an array of rustic folk art pieces are interesting finishing touches.

Left: *A strong color can make a beautiful and original statement. Here, bright amethyst walls are paired with crisp white cabinets and classic high-back island stools.*

Right: *Interesting cabinets, in this case, ones with unusual reeded panels, can be a big part of a kitchen's creative appeal. A neatly scaled range hood and an oval mirror on the backsplash add further interest in this kitchen. Dark-tiled countertops are practical and handsome and set off the white and colorful accessories to their best advantage.*

A handsome wood floor, cabinets, and refrigerator panel wrap the room in warmth, and the massive size of the fridge is nicely balanced by a trio of airy wicker-and-rattan counter stools. ***Refrigerator: Sub-Zero; oven: Miele; faucet: Grohe; sink: Elkay.***

PRACTICAL GOOD LOOKS with just a few surprises to shake things up—that's what eclectic kitchen design does best. Glass block is probably not the first material that comes to mind when you think of kitchen design, but this kitchen makes creative use of it. Framed in beautiful wood, glass block takes on a luster that's light-years away from industrial use. Because of its mass, the glass-block island dominates the scene, but the effect is exciting, not overwhelming. On the walls, a combination of rich cream and blue-violet creates exciting visual contrasts. This unusual wall treatment really works in this eclectic kitchen. Other eye-catching features include a custom-designed stainless-steel range hood and an angled custom backsplash with built-in condiment rack.

A glass-block island, lit from within, adds even more drama to a one-of-a-kind work island. The tiered unit includes a spacious curved snack counter plus a work station with drawers and display shelves aplenty. ***Designer: Kitchens & Baths by Louise Gilmartin. Cabinets: Heritage Custom Kitchens.***

Artistic Flair

HOW CAN YOU visually integrate a kitchen that's open to a great room or family room? Carrying through common treatments is probably the easiest way to make the two areas flow together attractively. This kitchen fronts onto a handsome, mostly contemporary-style family room, so it was important to cook up some visual excitement to match. To meet this need, elaborate, colorful custom tiles on the backsplash go beyond the usual simple patterns to create mosaic-style pictures. The colors in the tiles were carefully chosen to coordinate with hues highlighted in the family room. Soothing cream-colored cabinets in the kitchen visually extend the space, making the mosaic tile masterpiece really stand out. Underfoot, the bisque-colored stone tile flooring throughout the kitchen and family room serves to visually unite the two spaces.

Playful touches, like this custom dining table, carry the artistic, colorful mood throughout the living space. An unusual table like this is the perfect companion to the eclectic mix of furniture and design found throughout these rooms.

Ample seating at the island counter is roomier than you might expect in a kitchen this size. The above-island pot rack and oversize, stainless-steel range hood show that this kitchen, however attractive, is a real work space.

Colorful mosaic designs wind around this kitchen's backsplash, lending a decorative flair to the otherwise clean-cut space. The colors—rust-red, dark blue-violet, yellow, and aqua—echo the scheme in the adjacent family room.
Designer: Charles Cunniffe Architects.

A dynamic duo of island cabinets with marble tops and sinks make a practical pair of work stations that don't clutter up the room. Early-modern lampshades over one counter add a '30s flair as well as needed task lighting; the stainless pan-laden pot rack suspended over the other island is timeless. **Designer: Cantley and Company Inc.**

WHITE MARBLE COUNTERTOPS and white wood cabinets with traditional brass hardware make a great basis for a kitchen that delivers some real innovations. The most obvious is the massive two-level commercial-style range flanked by simple windows. The windows are the same height as the range, so the visual balance of "mass" is surprisingly right in this small space. Elsewhere in the room, the two relatively small counters each have a sink (or two), creating a pair of back-to-back prep counter work stations conveniently close to the range. A huge stainless fridge helps keep the stove from looking out of place, and a raft of clever storage solutions above eye level, from a traditional hanging pot rack to a TV cubby, adds to the overall functionality of the room. Bentwood armchairs with wicker seats and a couple of cabinets framed in natural wood lend a touch of warmth to all the white.

Repeated color notes pull the varying elements of the eclectic style into a coherent scheme. Naturally finished Bentwood chairs and several cupboard frames share the natural tones of the baskets and even the warm hues of the copper cookware. For all its soothing ambience, this kitchen is filled with clever storage, like the TV cubby and the slotted racks above the modern fridge that handle hard-to-store serving trays and pot lids.

Just Peachy

A SPACIOUS, HIGH-ceilinged room like this needs little adornment to be spectacular. Beautiful materials worthy of the space were used to create a lavish but not overly complex design. A big part of the delight of this room is the dishy color scheme. The deep coral tone of the red granite used on the countertops is echoed in two lighter shades of faux-finished coral and peach on the upper walls. Tumbled marble in a slightly pink-tinged taupe, punctuated with a ribbon of small black custom tiles, makes great-looking backsplashes. Pale taupe cabinets curve around corners to create a fascinating visual rhythm, and rows of suspended violet-colored lamps unite the upper and lower regions of the room. Postmodern-inspired niches in the upper wall also help tie the room together and give the homeowner a chance to display a few carefully chosen accessories.

Left: *Tiered countertops of highly polished red granite make a practical, great-looking work island/snack bar. The same granite covers the second island (opposite the range) as well as the perimeter counters.* ***Designer: Kitchens & Baths by Louise Gilmartin. Range: Wolf; lighting: Neidhardt and LBL.***

Soft colors—peach, coral, and soft taupe—keep this grandly scaled room from becoming overwhelming. Cabinets are placed to break up the space and offer a variety of closed and glassed-in cabinets at several heights. ***Cabinets: Heritage Custom Kitchens.***

Arts and Crafts Charm

A BRIGHT, CHEERFUL MIX of traditional, Arts and Crafts, and modern influences adds up to a friendly, great-looking kitchen. A traditionally styled dark-wood cooktop island acts as a visual stabilizer in the center of the space, while the white countertop keeps it bright. Double wall ovens are set in the same dark-wood cabinetry. Adding contrast, beautiful honey-toned pine cabinetry is embellished with wonderful Arts and Crafts carvings and strip moldings on the glass cabinet doors. Colorful mosaic tile designs on the backsplash combine the geometric with the natural or free-form and add a lighthearted touch. The workhorse fridge and in-island cooktop deliver performance without compromising the room's lyrical style. Cheery red-and-white oversize checkerboard tiles lend a retro feel and make the floor an exciting focal point in its own right.

Craftsmanship lives in this splendid yet supremely functional Arts and Crafts cabinetry. One cabinet houses the microwave; another features classic European-style plate racks. A corner sink with lots of food prep space on both sides helps make the most of every square inch. **Cabinets: Wood-Mode.**

Mix it up with dark and light cabinets for an Arts and Crafts look that celebrates hand-craftsmanship and one-of-a-kind designs. White countertops tie the two wood tones together. Suspended Arts and Crafts–style lamps at varying heights unite the upper planes of the room with the living level.
Designer: Lou Ann Bauer, Bauer Interior Design.

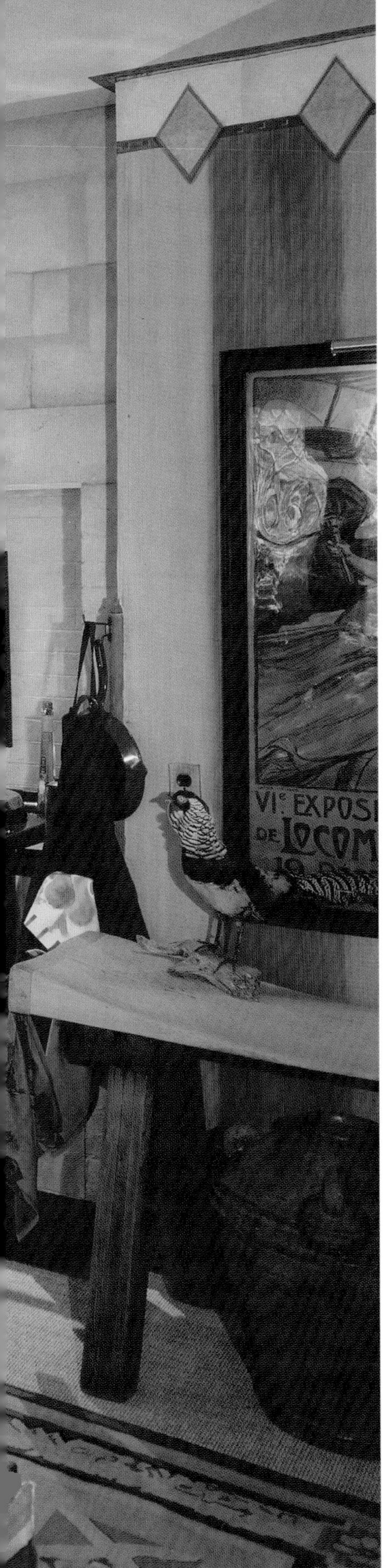

ARTISTIC EXPRESSION is all around this room. While the beautiful art glass and overall color scheme take center stage, the primitive pottery, art nouveau-era poster, traditional 19th-century oil painting, and fun mix of floral and patterned fabrics all state that someone with a fearless, eclectic point of view lives here. With spirited colors like lilac, green, and gold adding to the celebratory mood, the space makes good use of a variety of prints, fabrics, wall treatments, and shapes. Hanging, emerald-green lamps suggest a mysterious Orient Express environment that's pure fun today. An earthy element is added through bright fresh flowers and intricately twined grapevine. The homeowner's collection of green, purple, rose, and gold-colored art glass and porcelain is right at home when displayed on this table. Windows, some expressively curved and others with Gothic diamond-shape muntins, are an important part of this room's charmingly adventurous style.

Left: *Part art nouveau, part Bloomsbury style, this exuberant dining space will put anyone in a party mood. Gold and lilac, an unconventional variant of the complementary purple and yellow scheme, is a welcome change from more traditional color schemes. That alone reveals an independent, romantic, and regal mind-set.* **Designer: Judy King Antiques.**

Right: *This cozy round table with a colorfully patterned top seats four on funky, lilac slipcovered dining chairs. The whimsical grapevine-festooned light fixture and funky patterned slipcovers can be swapped for something more subdued, but the interesting windows and wall coverings work with many styles.*

Collections count in creating a unique, truly personal kitchen design. This room is blue because, from Meissen (German) Blue Onion to classic Chinese Blue Willow, this homeowner revels in blue-and-white china, and extra space is devoted to showcasing these collections.

BLUE AND WHITE has long been one of the most beloved color schemes for kitchens because it always looks clean and fresh. This kitchen is a quirky update on an old Dutch painting, with a collection of Delft and Chinese export porcelains prominently displayed. Furthering the look is the clever "art" arrangement of spice rack and still-life painting interspersed with decorative plates. Open built-in shelves allow for even more collectible china displays. Turn-of-the-century "golden oak" chairs, elaborately machine embossed, are vintage finds today and are charming for informal kitchen dining. To keep the look from being too sweet, ragged-finish plain cabinets with very contemporary wire drawer and door pulls add a cool note, and a classic large-checkered tablecloth and floor are boldly retro. Above the cabinets, an elaborate floral mural restates the traditional cottage theme. A custom-colored floral motif in ceramic tile makes the sink backsplash a small center of interest on its own.

Left: *Decorative treatments add extra visual interest. Cabinet doors have no panels but create a sense of depth nonetheless with an attractive ragged faux finish. Above the cabinets, a border of stylized flowers bloom. The sink backsplash features a brightly colored custom design of—what else?—flowers.*

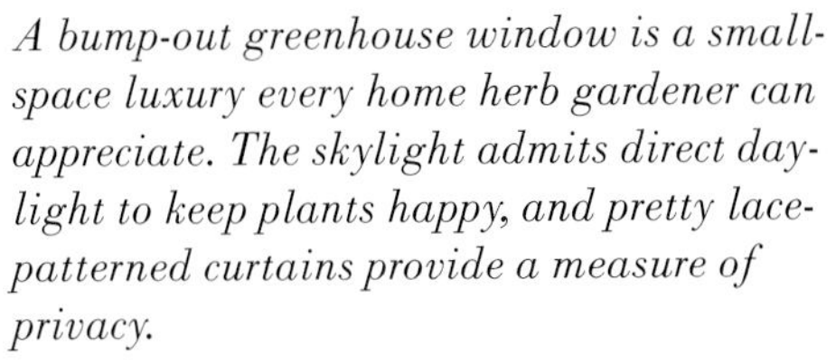

A bump-out greenhouse window is a small-space luxury every home herb gardener can appreciate. The skylight admits direct daylight to keep plants happy, and pretty lace-patterned curtains provide a measure of privacy.

Forecast: Bright and Breezy

Open to great views, this sun-washed kitchen owes much to the inspiration of a casually elegant beach house. Pale hues and generous amounts of light account for the breath-of-fresh-air ambience in a space that uses design motifs from several eras and styles. The driftwood-bleached cabinets with rope trim and pediment tops are very traditional, their dignity further enriched with mottled granite countertops. In contrast, contemporary-style windows and patio doors combine with exposed ceiling beams to create a space that seems even bigger than it is. Rustic stone tile flooring and a brick-accented island also contribute to the unusual mix—resulting in a very individualistic kitchen that feels like home but is also sophisticated and good-looking.

Left: *The angled island with inset cooktop and sink allows access from a variety of vantage points in the room. The rustic brick base complements the stone tile flooring, while both provide a welcome contrast to the traditional white cabinetry.* ***Designer: Betsey Meyer, CKD, CBD, Betsey Meyer Associates. Cabinets: Heritage Custom Kitchens.***

Right: *Natural-toned hues on the driftwood-bleached cabinetry add to the soothing ambience of this kitchen. The mottled granite countertop adds another pleasing, natural pattern to the setting. Traditional lighting fixtures offer a fresh contrast to the contemporary-style windows.*

LOADED WITH ARTISTIC PANACHE, this unusual kitchen, while not large, makes more than a few grand design gestures with a wealth of unique, luxurious elements. Two major units, the range and the island, are very eye-catching but also deliver high performance. The commercial-style range, backsplash, and vent hood in dazzling stainless steel dominate one wall; the striking kitchen island offers plenty of storage and food prep space. In contrast, black granite countertops and natural-finished knotty pine cabinets with unobtrusive wood knobs stay nicely in the background. Above the counters, a riot of richly colored hand-painted tiles makes a great backsplash, giving this room an artistic, one-of-a-kind flair. Above, traditional windows with real wood moldings are a subtle luxury the discerning eye appreciates. Inventive yet practical, this kitchen is clearly a fun place to be.

Rustic knotty-pine cabinets get a romantic, pale finish, in contrast to the backsplash's colorful array of handmade tiles. The tiles, all relatively small but in an interesting mix of sizes and shapes, are hand-painted in rich tones of lime, cobalt, gold, navy, teal, and brown.

Opposite: *The black-painted, black granite-topped island features traditional turned legs, and both the island and the stove are raised off the floor in the style of freestanding furniture. Practicality prevails in the island's display shelf and three dry goods bins behind glass-front drawers, while moon and star accents provide a bit of whimsy.*

KITCHENS

A BEAUTIFUL BARN is what this kitchen/dining/great room recalls, with all the reassuring images the barn idea carries. Scalloped-back maple chairs, an elaborate chandelier, and even a deer-head trophy definitely pay homage to the old days, but they work beautifully to relieve what might be starkness in the adjacent, more modern kitchen. The effect is unquestionably witty. The shell of the room is extraordinary, too; a great-room space with a high, exposed-beam ceiling and traditional windows that give it rustic barn proportions. The massively elegant white-painted mantel is totally traditional, as are the dining table and chairs, but on the kitchen side, shining stainless steel dominates the scene and injects contemporary brightness into the dramatically dark painted room.

Opposite: *A super-long countertop that divides the kitchen from the dining area goes to great lengths to house the homeowner's book collection in a novel way. Instead of tall bookcases, these low shelves keep favorites within reach of the table. It's enough to make anyone want to read at mealtime.*

Right: *Taking a shine to high performance, this galley kitchen features a commercial-style stove and dazzling stainless-steel backsplash and range hood. A pair of refrigerators flank the stove area for maximum storage and convenience. The sink, with a very traditional gooseneck faucet, is set directly across from the stove, creating a tightly efficient triangle despite the extended length of the room.* **Range: Caldera Corp.**

English Cottage

Charming, romantic, and comfortable, English cottage style is one of the world's most endearing—and enduring—styles. More romantic than traditional style, more polished than American farmhouse style, the English look features a relaxed air with a touch of whimsy. Whether your interpretation is the cozy cottage look or the more spacious farmhouse/country house look, you'll love the traditional, timeless elements.

To create the look, use crisp white cut-work curtains, fine porcelain, and comfy cushions paired with high-backed wooden chairs, tall stools, and fine old (or old-looking) hardwood tables. Specify fine-grained hardwood cabinets (some with leaded-glass fronts), marble or faux-marble countertops, and flooring of slate, small black-and-white ceramic tiles, or wood. English style is a natural for freestanding furniture, from china cabinets to tea carts, and a mix of formal and rustic antiques. And it revels in garden motifs—especially roses, violets, and

ivy—on wallcoverings, window valances, seat cushions, and china patterns. Lavish floral chintzes in a riot of garden colors bring the English garden indoors. (Select a mix of chintzes with one or two colors in common but with differently scaled patterns.) Except where safety near the stove is an issue, indulge in balloon shades, ruffled or swagged valances and curtains, and cushions with bows on chairs and counter stools. For an extra-homey touch, try the surprise of a needlepoint footstool or other small upholstered piece in the dining area of the kitchen.

English cottage kitchen furniture goes way back, so Jacobean or even Gothic styles, as well as graceful Queen Anne and Victorian English pieces, are right at home, all together. English cottage style also takes to fresh colors: tea-rose, cantaloupe, robin's-egg blue, and buttercream paired with lettuce- or celadon-green. Add a fireplace, a brass teakettle, crisp white table linens, and a white trellis for pink roses outside the door. What could be more inviting?

Tasteful and Pretty

A MIX OF CLOSED and display cabinets, plus open shelving and a convenient wine rack, create interesting variety without sacrificing a unified look. This principle works just as well—or perhaps even better—in a small kitchen as in this spacious one. Storage aplenty and a visually simplified design help retain the charm of English cottage style without the clutter. Traditionally styled cabinetry in white sets a spacious, restful scene. Even the range hood and ceramic-tile backsplash are as pristinely white as possible. Snowy linens (lace-edged tablecloth, napkins, and tea towel) carry out the theme. The sink island, too, is white, with plenty of open shelves to display silver and other fine serving pieces. Tucked up against the island, in a traditional version of the dining peninsula, a vintage wooden table with handsome turned legs keeps company with four skirted slipper chairs. These chairs, along with the candlestick lamps on the table, set the white, rose, and green color scheme that makes this kitchen so inviting. At teatime or any time, this delectable setting welcomes friends for a chat or an evening of fine dining.

Left: *Setting a charming table is easy in a workable kitchen like this one. A vintage table and rose-print slipcovered chairs lend a sense of comfortable informality and pampering any guest is bound to appreciate. The adjacent work island, set perpendicular to the table, makes serving extra treats a breeze.* ***Designer: Kitchen Design Studio of New Canaan, Inc.***

Right: *In this romantic white kitchen, the black and stainless-steel tones introduced by the wall oven and cooktop aren't jarring because they're balanced with black countertops throughout.* ***Cabinets: Premier Custom Built Cabinets.***

BREAD

Paintbox Charmer

It's possible that a kitchen filled with wood cabinets and a black commercial-style stove might get a bit claustrophobic, but not this one. The savvy homeowner pulled out a bunch of paintbox colors, predominantly rosy red, green, and yellow, to create a lighthearted mood. Lots of white, a never-fail recipe for freshness, makes the colors really stand out. Narrow strip flooring, whitewashed and distressed, adds more vintage appeal. Glass cathedral-style cabinet doors are given a fresh look with gathered green fabric. Curtains in a cheerful yellow print capture sunshine, and decorative border tiles around the perimeter of the countertops add another charming cottage touch. An old-time butcher's block adds extra work space and a great rustic look to this cottage-style kitchen. A cheery dining nook is easy to create with a few design tricks. To maximize the window's importance, hang the curtain just below the ceiling. To define the dining space, find an interesting suspended lighting fixture.

Left: *Shirred fabric is a charmingly old-fashioned look that's easy to achieve: Just gather the fabric onto short curtain rods mounted at the top and bottom of the cabinet glass.*

The dining nook gains importance from a handsome antique china cabinet, a wall rack filled with emerald-green glassware, and another sunny window curtained in the same yellow fabric found in the kitchen's work space.

A Country Romance

DELECTABLE STYLE like this depends on the many small artistic touches that signal a creative homeowner lives here. To start, the room has the low-beamed ceiling of a classic cottage. There are also plenty of rustic touches, including a terra-cotta tile floor. Decorative hand-painted tiles in contemporary patterns and colors, a big part of the room's appeal, are everywhere, from the floor to the range hood. The mix of rustic and artistic continues in the cabinetry, which is made of knotty pine but features traditional detailing and a soft whitewashed color. Ivy-painted white dining chairs are just right for this lighthearted room, as is the deft touch of patterned fabric cushions on the counter stools. A double sink in the island, built-in microwave, and wood-paneled fridge deliver performance without disturbing the gentle ambience.

Left: *The roomy island's rustic brick endposts are softened by a rope-trimmed edge and pretty hand-decorated tiles on top. Seat cushions covered in a frisky print enhance the garden ambience.* ***Designer: Gail Drury, CKD, CBD, Drury Designs, LTD.***

Right: *Hand-painted ceramic door and drawer pulls on the whitewashed, beaded knotty pine cabinetry echo the charming decorative tiles scattered throughout the kitchen. A bright blue stove adds a jolt of excitement to the gentle color scheme.*

Coming up Roses

Below: *A balloon-shaded window under a cherry-wood bridge between cabinets makes a fine focal point. While the flowered tiles are rather special, the overall look is accessible for big budgets or small, thanks to a great array of coordinating wallcoverings and window treatments. Floral porcelains, too, are plentiful at all price points.*

ENGLAND'S WEATHER, perpetually cool and moist, gives it some of the world's most beautiful flowers, including roses the size of cabbages. Chintz fabrics, first brought from the colony of India, were perfect for capturing the essence of the English garden and bringing it indoors. English country houses, often filled with beautifully carved but dark wood paneling, bloomed with the bright, informal prettiness of flowers on white grounds. Here, dark mahogany or walnut paneling is replaced by rich cherry cabinets, and roses are everywhere; floral fabrics, porcelains, and botanical printed tiles are just some of the ways roses star in this charming kitchen. Key to the look is a mix of prints in small, medium, and large scales, but with a consistent array of colors.

Opposite: *Roses are abloom everywhere in this kitchen, from the wallcovering, window treatment, dishes, and decorative tiles to the vases filled with—you guessed it—roses. Here, it's true rose and pale pink on a white background; appealing alternatives could be Staffordshire porcelain-blue roses on white, or yellow and peach roses on an ivory background.* ***Designer: JoAnne Welsh.***

Subtle Wit and Charm

Some elements of English style go back nearly a thousand years, so it's no wonder the appealing style that flourished in prewar Britain included influences of Gothic and Tudor styles, among others. This kitchen deftly incorporates such elements for a look that's extraordinary, yet seems as familiar as a storybook. Cabinets with leaded glass doors are a winsome touch, and the tall support risers, curved like Queen Anne-style chair splats, are both elegant and charming. The tile floor with the timeworn, soft-edged look of tumbled marble in a mix of ruddy hues makes a nice contrast to the pristine white cabinets. In the midst of these subtle white and tawny shades, a glorious copper range hood brings in a strong note of warmth and luxury, while the no-nonsense black countertops add snap. The drop-in, porcelain-aproned sink, white Venetian blinds, and banker's-style drawer pulls are examples of old-fashioned elements whose utility and appeal seem timeless.

Left: *Leaded glass-front cabinets evoke romantic Tudor style, the uniquely tall support risers suggest a gingerbread cottage, and both hearken back to a neo-Gothic style that reigned in prewar Britain. The look is a standout, but in a very livable way.* ***Designer: Karen Richmond, CKD, CBD, Neil Kelly Designers/Remodelers.***

Right: *A gleaming stainless-steel stove and sparkling copper range hood might overwhelm in some spaces, but in this remarkably designed room, they're simply exciting. A tumbled-marble backsplash with a subtle star motif maintains the low-key but rich look.*

RED, BLACK, AND WHITE, a perennially popular kitchen color scheme, takes on an elegant yet not too serious look in this English country kitchen. Traditionally styled cabinets with arched cathedral doors and brass pulls offer ample storage in the compact space, while a matching island provides sufficient work space. The wood has a pickled finish: whitewash applied, then wiped off, for a casual look. The window treatment, often a challenge in kitchens, is worth noting: A classical white arch is reframed in raspberry, then bisected by a swag in a raspberry-red neoclassical print. The same type of lavish print appears in the black wallpaper border above the cupboards. A small, curlicued hanging lamp above the island is one more little touch in a room whose charm is made up of many small delights.

A richly carved wood range hood stays in the country mode with a pickled finish. Glass-front cupboards decked with checked fabric are a cheerful touch. Plain white ceramic tiles, applied on the diagonal, make a nice background for a variety of accessories.

Opposite: *The ornate wallpaper border—traditional bows and garlands in red, white, gold, and green on black—lends a formal note to this country kitchen, as does the draped, swagged length of glorious red fabric framing the window.*

Left: *A built-in microwave nestles above the built-in conventional oven to create a cooking center. The small island, constructed with traditional corbels supporting the countertop, offers suitable landing space for hot cookware from the ovens and is scaled just right for the space.*

Capturing the Sunlight

OPEN TO AN AIRY dining nook and blessed with a good-size window of its own, this kitchen is filled with sunlight. The cheerful setting is enhanced by the color scheme of blue, white, and soft yellow. This neat space houses everything a pair of cooks could want: A double sink and dishwasher are stationed on the window wall; the island houses the cooktop and another sink. A few whimsical touches go a long way toward creating a lighthearted mood. For example, curving vines carved into some of the cabinet corners and a blue rope-motif countertop edging are pretty details. An unusual window fabric carries the color scheme in mini-Austrian shades that are opulent but not overwhelming. Traditional glass-and-brass light fixtures in the kitchen and coordinating ceiling fan lights in the dining area continue the gleam into the evening. Day or night, the mood is welcoming and creative.

Left: *The unusually shaped island houses both the cooktop and an additional sink, making it easy for two cooks to work together.* ***Designer: Gary White, CKD, CBD, CID, Kitchen & Bath Design.***

Right: *Traditional cabinetry gets a playful touch with curling vines and floral accents carved here and there. The countertop edges in white-bordered blue add another casual, painterly accent and further the room's color scheme. Glass-front cabinets make a perfect home for blue-and-white English china.*

Timeless Comforts

An impressive built-in china cabinet centers on a traditional European plate rack beneath a heavily carved traditional front. Tall, narrow glass-front cabinets house even more of the homeowner's prized china collection.

A SERIES OF ANGLES defines this striking kitchen that gains more importance with its handsome cabinets. Traditional scrolled corbels accent the stove area, which is flanked by open shelves displaying colorful crockery and china. A black wrought-iron utensil rack offers even more open storage—a hallmark of country style. In some kitchens, every square foot would be taken up with cabinets, but this one leaves enough open wall space to give a little breathing room. The wallcovering, a stone-textured ivory overlaid with subtle, antique-gold stripes, coordinates nicely with the wood cabinets and white moldings. A cozy dining nook exudes both comfort and style with armchairs for each diner and richly colored fabric valances topping the windows and French doors.

Right: *Collections, important to any traditional country look, shine here. Copper pans, small artworks, colorful china and stoneware, an antique tea chest on a stand, and an array of potted plants, including traditional English primroses, all add up to a charming space.* ***Designer: Terri Ervin, Decorating Den Interiors.***

Left: *The adjacent dining nook shares in the kitchen's country spirit with armchairs at each place and a quilt as a casual tablecloth. A Tiffany-style pendant lamp and jewel-toned floral fabric valances over the windows and French doors add elegant touches.*

Balloon shades and a swagged valance make the most of a great bay window. A cozy window seat with coordinating pillows adds extra seating at the table. Small-print wallpaper that unites the walls and ceiling visually expands the room. **Refrigerator: Sub-Zero.**

A ROMANTIC COUNTRY KITCHEN comes to life with a wealth of small, inventive decorating touches. The basics are gracefully traditional without being too fancy: Cathedral-door cabinets in a medium wood tone and low-luster finish go well with traditional wheat-backed chairs and a friendly round table. White-ceramic-tile countertops and backsplashes are embellished with pretty floral motifs. Top-of-the-line appliances, including a range with a built-in grill and a generously sized, side-by-side fridge, deliver serious performance, but the decorative details are what really make this room so charming. Ruffled Austrian balloon shades and window seat cushions in a soft red-and-white-checked print give picnic appeal to the dining nook and create a special look over the sink backsplash. A stylized floral stencil that repeats throughout the room helps tie the wood pieces together and subtly underscores the pretty country look.

For a fun backsplash treatment, this gilt-framed vignette topped with an Austrian balloon shade creatively gives the illusion of depth similar to a window. Narrow shelves bisecting the backsplash add convenient extra storage.
Designer: Penny Chin, Elements In Design.

A custom design of colorful flowers on the tile countertop edges and the range backsplash gives a lighthearted garden touch to this romantic kitchen.
Range: Viking.

A MIX OF GOLDEN woods, tawny granite, white-painted woods, and wrought iron lends an informally elegant air to this appealing kitchen. While the cabinetry and woodwork are definitely traditional, several of the other elements are refreshingly contemporary: the open layout; the mix of painted and stained woods; the stainless-steel stove, range hood, sink, and dishwasher; and the cove-lit, recessed ceiling. The key to this space is the use of similar honey-color tones in stone and wood. Even the fruit-printed Roman shades over the generous windows and the coordinating seat cushion fabric add a quietly opulent accent. In contrast, the softly lit ceiling and the white-painted cabinetry help open the space up, and the wrought-iron garden chairs add a breath of fresh air. From the breakfast peninsula, diners can easily see the TV enclosed behind built-in traditional cabinet doors in the adjoining family room. This is a kitchen that's easy to work in, easy on the eyes, and timelessly romantic.

Above: *A handsome peninsula with a round granite top and a base paneled to match the traditional cabinetry makes a spacious breakfast spot. Wrought-iron counter-high chairs create a garden ambience and coordinate with the classic iron chandelier over the nearby dining table.*

Right: *Honey-toned kitchen cabinetry looks great teamed with white cabinets and bookshelves in the adjoining space. A paneled side-by-side fridge, built-in oven, microwave, and wine cooler all fit nicely along the kitchen peninsula.*

Opposite: *Tawny granite countertops, golden wood cabinets, and a pretty fruit-patterned Roman shade create a warm, homey mood. The recessed ceiling with cove lighting adds brightness and a contemporary design note.* ***Designer: Lila Levinson, ASID, CKD, CID, Accent On Design.***

Euro-Modern

FOR A KITCHEN on the cutting edge, think Euro-modern. First created in city loft homes, this savvy style serves up drama without fuss in homes of every kind. To get the look, help yourself to lots of sophisticated black, preferably in granite or ceramic tile (polished for easy-clean walls, matte for no-slip flooring). Investigate the latest technologies for high-performance cooking, clean-up, and recycling, many of which originated with European manufacturers and product designers.

Don't be afraid to show a lot of metal, especially stainless steel. Mixed metals are a confident Euro-style signature, so take that brushed or shiny stainless steel and spark it with copper, iron, chrome, or brass. Specify frameless Euro-style cabinets in smooth-grained wood, either as dark as mahogany or as pale as birch. If you prefer, have something custom made in a handsome laminate, perhaps in an adventurous pattern. For the sleekest look, select a cabinet style with finger grooves instead of pulls for an unbro-

ken plane of color, or, for an individual touch, choose cabinets with modern, statement-making hardware. Use glass, especially clear and green-tinted, in interesting ways, perhaps as a decorative inset in a backsplash or counter edge. Choose granite, tile, or laminate countertops in black or charcoal-gray. Add a space-saving breakfast bar with black leather stools or a brushed-steel-and-glass dining table with classic modern chairs in black.

For accent colors, go for something rich and different: retro-green, teal or violet-blue, or lush cantaloupe. Or, if you desire a more "traditional" Euro-modern look, chill a nice white and warm up with a great red: Both look great with black. Accessories are ultra-modern or infused with a slightly mysterious chic that recalls the '30s, '40s, or '50s. Dramatic and confident, Euro-modern makes a sophisticated statement that's just your style.

Cool Blue

Here, black granite and shiny metal gleam brightly. Black countertops are edged with thin bands of chrome; stainless wall plates, range hood, and pot rack are set off by the wall-high black granite backsplash.

SPACE-AGE DAZZLE is everywhere in this bright, sharp, rigorously modern kitchen. No wasted space, no extra decorative elements, just planes of bright metal and color to enliven the room. Stark steel-silver and black are the predominant colors, but the room takes a dramatic departure when it comes to the oven. An intense cobalt-blue, the oven is the room's exciting focal point. A similar effect could be achieved with fire-engine red or another strong color, since today's commercial-quality cooking appliances have entered the fashion arena. Setting off the bold blue color, shining stainless-steel cabinets flank the oven top and bottom, and the stainless-steel range hood and pot rack contrast brightly with the dramatic black granite backsplash. Underfoot, naturally finished wood plank flooring adds a warm touch to this otherwise starkly modern room.

Left: *Stainless-steel cabinets, some with solid doors, others with frosted-glass doors, fit in smoothly among stainless-steel-fronted appliances, sink, and drop-in cooktop.*

Opposite: *Two extra-large skylights flood the room with light that reflects off the stainless-steel cabinetry. A sharply angled snack counter gives the kitchen a bit of extra floor space; a pair of stools fits snugly underneath.*

Artistic License

Left: *Outside of the cutting-edge cooking area, rustic colors prevail. Above the two-tiered sink counter, naturally finished wood shelves display a collection of rustic cinnabar, gold, and olive-green pottery; a pair of woven rattan chairs adds more natural warmth.*

NOT EVERYONE would have the courage to install a royal purple stove, let alone matching cabinets, but in this fun and modern kitchen, the look is spectacularly successful. An equally bold acid-green panel backs up the sculpturesque range hood. The look works because the spots of strong color are balanced by larger areas of calm neutrals: naturally finished wood upper cabinets and wood strip flooring, plus pale gray granite and ceramic tile countertops and backsplash. This kind of balance lets frisky colors deliver a sense of fun and creativity (a perfect inspiration for cooking up something new) without a hectic or over-the-top effect. The dramatic color combination is the perfect backdrop for a uniquely modern yet comfortable work space. Check out the double wall oven tucked into a corner wall: This makes extremely efficient use of an otherwise wasted space.

Left: *A big stainless-steel refrigerator contrasts with a tier of open pantry shelves to take the best of both old and new. The fridge also ties in with the shiny surface of the custom range hood.*

Theatrical Lighting

THIS MODERN KITCHEN is all gleaming surfaces, but it's also warm and welcoming: That's the genius of this space. Special touches of modern-style elegance are apparent everywhere. Custom-designed maple cabinets are naturally finished to show the fine grain. Horizontal lines, a hallmark of contemporary style, are emphasized here with black banding that runs the width of the cabinets. Granite makes a handsome countertop and adds a bit of natural pattern to the clean lines of the room. There's plenty of seating at the two-tiered sink counter, as well as in the adjacent dining nook. Lighting, often handled simply with a series of recessed cans, is a major design element in this room. A trio of attractive suspended fixtures over the counter impart a vaguely Eastern, exotic look, and the circular fixture over the dining table is definitely out of this world. Most interesting, however, is the cove lighting that defines the dining area, lending a sense of special occasion to any gathering.

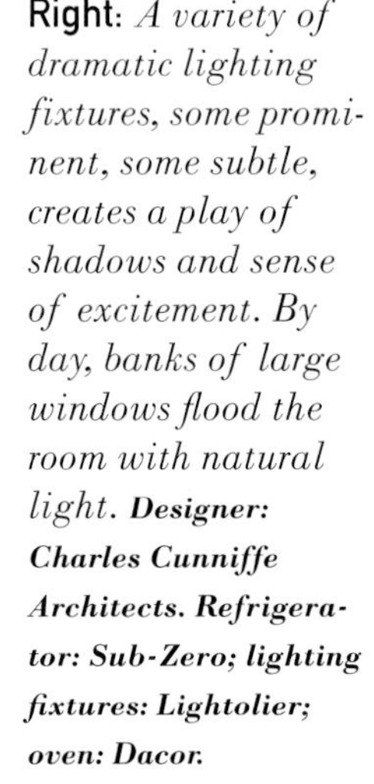

Right: *A variety of dramatic lighting fixtures, some prominent, some subtle, creates a play of shadows and sense of excitement. By day, banks of large windows flood the room with natural light.* ***Designer: Charles Cunniffe Architects. Refrigerator: Sub-Zero; lighting fixtures: Lightolier; oven: Dacor.***

Left: *The maple cabinets, counter base, and dining table shine with natural beauty. Black accents, found in the bands running through the cabinetry, the Italian modern counter stools, and the Op Art–inspired chair fabric, add snap to the design.*

Bright Light, Big City

THESE MODERN-LOVING HOMEOWNERS craved light in their kitchen, so two narrow windows were installed on the end wall to flank the gleaming stainless-steel stove and range hood. Glossy maple laminate reflects the abundance of daylight and presents a sleek interior. The countertop, a very dark green, features large particles of pale minerals and flecks of gold that sparkle in the sunlight. The floor's rich wood tones visually anchor the pale cabinetry and balance the dark countertops. To maximize storage space, there's a pull-out pantry next to the fridge, roll-out shelves in the base cabinets, deep pot drawers, and a swing-out unit in a corner cabinet. The central location of the island allows for traffic to flow freely on all sides.

Opposite: *A mixed-use island incorporates three different surface heights for a variety of tasks. On the eating-area side, the surface is desk height and is accompanied by a small wood cabinet to hide clutter. A countertop surface perches on top of the wooden drawers, providing a perfect place for serving.* ***Design: Sieguzi Interior Designs, Inc. Cabinets: SieMatic Corp.***

Additional storage space, a much-needed feature in this kitchen, was provided by two demi-tall pantries added to the eating area. The design includes basalt-gray laminate wall panels with stainless-steel studs and curved, thick glass shelves that echo the shape of the granite table.

Colorful Options

METAL CABINETS, shunned in period or country design schemes, are celebrated in Euro-modern style, and for good reason: Nothing else responds so well to designers' creative color play. Cool laminate-front cabinets are at home in super-modern spaces because the color and design range are virtually limitless. These two kitchens illustrate the point perfectly, as colored cabinetry takes center stage. In one kitchen, yellow cabinets as pale as Italian ice cozy up to a retro-style fridge and state-of-the-art cooktop/range hood/oven unit. A swath of soft apricot defines the appliance wall, and the color is repeated in the kicky light fixtures. In the other kitchen, rich cobalt-blue base cabinets are a splendid foil to white upper cabinets and naturally finished wood flooring. Crimson-red dining chairs balance the blue and inject a note of warmth. In both cases, surprisingly colored cabinets create a look that delights.

Right: *Lemon and orange sorbet colors on a cabinet unit, a wall, and lighting fixtures partner with industrial cement and stainless steel in this cutting-edge, Italian-modern kitchen. The stainless cooktop/range hood/oven unit's silvery tones tie in the polished cement floor.* ***Cabinets: Valcucine USA.***

Right: *Intense crimson and blue create an exciting contrast to neutral white, steel, and wood tones in this eye-catching kitchen. A dramatic cylindrical range hood becomes a shining sculptural focal point.* ***Cabinets: Downsview Kitchens.***

A strictly minimalist ethic has tremendous potential for drama, as shown here. A two-story kitchen confines the under-counter oven, inset cooktop, and sink to one wall. The drama is heightened—literally—by the open feel of the room as the walls turn to glass and open to the second floor.

THERE ARE ALMOST as many types of modern design from which to choose as there are traditional, and a modern afficionado knows the difference. While soft contemporary and modern based on the work of Frank Lloyd Wright are familiar and popular, other modern styles are pioneering the look of tomorrow. One kitchen here demonstrates the minimalist ethic: a look that shuns all nonessential design elements, accessories, and ornamentation. Storage is a top priority in this style because clutter has no place in a scheme where the goal is a pervading sense of coolness and total calm. In the other kitchen, playfulness, even rebelliousness, clearly prevails. Color is used with abandon for its ability to excite emotion. Shapes are often curved rather than angled, and natural motifs, like the moon-shape cooktop and range hood shown here, are employed whenever the engineering allows it. This design says the future may be unknown, but it may also turn out to be fun.

Gleaming cobalt-blue cabinetry, punctuated by a black range with a demi-lune-shape cooktop and its quarter-moon-shape range hood, demonstrate the courageous artistry that has made Italian design the world leader in modern style. ***Cabinets: Snaidero USA.***

A Slice of Style

Clean-lined and striking but also friendly and soothing, this kitchen offers the best of both worlds. Not content with that, it throws in a few surprising design curves to make you sit up and take notice. Take the focal-point island: While most kitchen islands treat the work and snack surfaces the same, this one uses black granite on the work top and then goes one better with a surprising frosted-glass top on the curved counter. The range's sculptural, shiny-bright look is a handsome foil to all the light wood surfaces. A stepped, curved ceiling houses recessed lighting and underscores the island counter's distinctive curved shape. Ample under-counter task lighting is more than practical: It also adds a balancing row of light in what could be the darker perimeter areas. The result of all this masterful planning is a space that's easy to work in as well as easy on the eyes.

Left: *Pale wood tones on the cabinets and floor make this modern kitchen a soothing place to be. Dark countertops offer a subtly rich note of color; the super-modern range and hood add a giant jolt of shine.* ***Designer: Erica Westeroth, XTC Design, Inc. Cabinets: Neff Kitchens.***

Left: *Exciting curves define this unusual countertop made of frosted glass over wood. The lower tier of the counter, topped in patterned black granite, houses the sink. A pair of chrome-trimmed glass trays suspended by a stainless-steel pole adds a sparkling, eye-catching touch.*

Glorious Geometry

WHILE MODERN STYLE owes a lot to squared-off shapes, these two rooms feature an interesting mix of sharp angles and rolling curves. Custom cabinetry in honeyed burl wood, a continental favorite, stars in both kitchens. With this foundation, each kitchen combines different elements to create elegant custom looks. In one, a speckled granite countertop adds visual excitement; in the other, a dark granite countertop creates a rich look. On one floor, luxuriously mottled gray marble tiles are cut with black diamond accent tiles for further pattern play. On the other, polished wood planks the same color as the cabinets create a soothing look. An arched window over the sink in one kitchen echoes the arched window wall of the nearby dining room/sunroom. The other room's window shape is repeated in its adjoining doorway frames. The look is masterful and witty—clearly Euro-modern.

Right: *An oven inset into one wing of this remarkable island redefines the work triangle. Black leather chairs and counter stools are comfortable and visually dramatic next to the mellow honey-toned wood on the cabinets and floor.* ***Manufacturer: Canac Kitchens.***

Right: *A handsome stainless-steel backsplash and range hood and a bow-front sink cabinet transform workaday elements into sculptural design statements. Fun metal counter stools in an attractive sunburst design are a witty finishing touch.* ***Manufacturer: Canac Kitchens.***

Thoroughly Modern Milieu

THE TRIED-AND-TRUE modern mix of warm, unadorned woods and shiny black counters and accents works exceptionally well in this kitchen. White walls and retro white linoleum tiles balance the mix and lighten up the look. A unit with upper and base cabinets acts as a room divider at one end, providing ample storage on the kitchen side. This kitchen isn't afraid to do things a little differently. For example, two stainless-steel sinks of different sizes and two different faucets, one with a built-in spray attachment, sit side by side instead of on different counters. The island, too, follows its own rules. Instead of the usual long, lean counter, this one's a neat little cube that doesn't overwhelm the space. It takes some sophisticated planning to come up with a scheme this clean and simple, but the results are clearly worth it.

Left: *Despite its compact size, this petite island houses a microwave oven and lots of storage compartments and makes a welcome spot for food prep or presentation.* **Right:** *A stainless-steel double oven and commercial-style gas cooktop fit smoothly into this run of beautifully engineered, modern cabinets. Looking more like executive office furniture than ordinary kitchen cabinets, these fit the modern aesthetic with minimalist drawer pulls and plain fronts that let the warm woodgrain star.*

French Country

HEARTY AND VERSATILE, yet oh so charming, French country is always in vogue. Not surprisingly, given France's reputation for world-class cuisine, it's especially appealing in the kitchen. To create this romantic style, select wood cabinets with the cool midtones of pecan or fruit-wood, or a faux-bois finish. For a small kitchen or one that pulls out all the stops for romance, you might even choose an antique-white wood finish. Whatever the cabinet tones, specify traditional cathedral-topped, raised-panel cabinet doors and antique brass pulls. For visual interest, mix solid-door and glass-door cupboards with open shelving. If you need extra storage, the armoire, a venerable French piece, is the perfect solution and also creates the traditional look of freestanding furniture. Dining groups may be compact little bistro affairs in metal, or they may be generously scaled in wood to host an extended family. French country furniture is distinctively curvy and pretty without being fussy, so you'll love to collect occasional chairs for extra guests.

The French are famous for their fine cookware, especially in copper, and there's no more beautiful, prestigious kitchen accessory than a wrought-iron-and-brass pot rack festooned with copper cookpots. A stove alcove is a great luxury, and a copper range hood is de rigueur. For color and practical beauty, terra-cotta floor tiles evoke the warmth of

Provence, while hand-painted wall tiles and murals celebrate French artistry. For fabrics, choose traditional Provençal prints in cheery yellow, royal blue, and brick-red. Or, if you love French art as much as French cooking, opt for a print inspired by the palettes of Impressionist or Expressionist paintings, perhaps in vibrant yellow-green, violet-blue, and coral.

This is the place to indulge your gourmet flair with wine racks, in-wall ovens, and marble countertops for rolling pastry. Haute cuisine or hot dogs, c'est si bon!

A Romantic Crusade

FOR SOMEONE who can't forget a visit to France's lovely cathedral towns (or for anyone who just wants to re-create the ambience), this kitchen is captivating. A beautiful, medievally inspired mosaic mural makes an extraordinary backsplash in a kitchen that exudes European romance. The range hood, ornately carved and shingled, is the perfect frame for the mural. Furthering the theme, a trio of leaded casement windows overlooks a black-slate double sink. Dark, traditionally carved cabinets with granite countertops and a butcher-block table with turned legs provide ample work space without sacrificing the antique look. For extra storage, a charming plate rack and pair of small cabinets with leaded glass doors do the job nicely. Underfoot, scatter rugs bearing designs inspired by medieval tapestries add a subtly colorful touch.

Right: *Lattice-insert base cabinets add a subtle garden reference that fits well into this French country kitchen. Ditto the dried herbs in the window, a hallmark of French cooking. The black-slate double sink and backsplash set off the curvy vintage faucet.*

Far right: *An overhead pot rack, a fixture in kitchens of many styles, looks perfect here, especially suspended over the impressive island—a combination of beauty and function in the center of the room.* ***Designer: Jim Dove, Canterbury Design Kitchen Interiors.***

FRENCH COUNTRY STYLE, often expressed with a riot of brilliantly colored fabrics, can also be cool, clean, and uncluttered, as shown here. A massive island running almost the entire length of the kitchen is just a step away from the paneled fridge, the sink, and the commercial-style range. A mix of closed and glass-door cabinets, plus a clever corner unit with small spice drawers, offers ample storage on the perimeter wall. The island also features numerous drawers and cupboards and a wine storage unit, so it's easy to keep the work space neat—a highly sought-after virtue in any kitchen. The color scheme, edited to white and wood tones with a touch of traditional French blue, also contributes to the fresh ambience. Overhead, the pot rack hung with dried flowers adds a creative, personal touch. Très chic!

Opposite: *White walls and cabinets give this kitchen a spacious look. Small blue ceramic tiles in the backsplash subtly tie in with the blue-and-white dining nook scheme. The crisp French look is enhanced by a pair of cushioned Napoleon-backed counter stools.*

Above: *One grandly scaled island offers plenty of room for one or more cooks. The handsome footed piece features a rich array of traditional carved details and decorative paneling as well as ample space for wine storage.*

Left: *A bay-window nook makes a lovely dining spot. Draperies and upholstered chairs in blue and white echo the colors and mood of the homeowner's china collection. A round, antique-gate-legged table and Windsor chairs enrich the pedigreed look.*

Romantic Details

Below: *Dark gray marble tops the kitchen island as well as the counters (see other photo) to create a continuity that sets off the room's lively details. An unusual stainless-steel sink and faucet are artful elements as well as practical ones.*

GUESTS ENTER this kitchen through a stone archway that signals something special is cooking. The center of attention is cabinetry in two pale tones enriched with subtle curves and classic rope detailing. The carved pediment above the stove conceals the range hood and provides housing for dramatic downlights. The backsplash is a literal work of art: a custom hand-painted still life of bread sticks, wine, and flowers, all rendered on ceramic tile. The island also adds to the romantic country look. Deeply paneled, with plenty of open display storage as well as closed cabinets, it's stained to suggest the heirloom look of a freestanding piece of antique furniture. Random-width plank flooring continues the vintage look. Windows are covered with a combination of lower shutters, painted to match the cabinets, and a flounced valance decked with ball fringe. It's a look that's pretty, just a bit frivolous, and very French.

Opposite: *An antique-looking island and cabinets that resemble fine furniture mean there's no need to close off this kitchen from the adjacent dining room. A curvaceous, chrome-and-brass chandelier over the work island adds a fun, opulent touch.*

THIS KITCHEN pulls out all the stops with an atmosphere that suggests the pleasures of an open-air pavilion. Ornate scrolled millwork and classic columns embrace specific areas of the room, setting them off from one another. This unusual treatment creates a sense of occasion on an everyday basis. Malachite-green marble countertops with a traditional ogee edge add timeless opulence and are a perfect pairing with the abundance of texture, color, and pattern found on the floor, ceiling, and walls. Within this festive environment, French practicality reigns. Flanking the cooktop, which is set in an eye-catching tiled niche, is a double wall oven to the left and refrigerator to the right. Just a few steps away, the island, framed in coordinating scrollwork and columns, houses all the amenities needed for easy hospitality. The artistically ragged walls in a glowing peach tone help complete this luxurious French country idyll.

Opposite: *The riot of colorfully flowered tiles on the cooktop's backsplash is complemented by the stylized patterns on the overhead ceiling tiles as well as the patterned marble floor tiles.*

Left: *A flourish of floral tiles evokes the timeless tile artistry of Provence. Narrow border tiles in complementary patterns and colors edge shelves that hold spices near the cooktop.*

Above: *Pavilion-style columns are both luxurious and lighthearted, creating a sense of occasion and separating the kitchen from the adjacent breakfast room. An under-counter wine cooler and dishwasher flank the sink cabinet.*

An Open Invitation

A walk-in pantry flanked by glass-front cabinets provides a luxury of storage (as well as a neat spot to stash the dog dish). The pantry/cabinet unit is unified by pretty, carved upper molding. Artful touches—a hand-painted bistro chair, straw hats—add a romantic air.

A FINE BAY WINDOW wrapping around the entire end wall is a distinctive focal point of this gracious kitchen. Making the most of the light, cabinets follow the lines of the wall in both directions. Opposite the sink cabinet, an island with turned legs, small open display shelves, and charming carved detailing evokes the look of freestanding furniture while housing a second sink. Black granite countertops, highly polished, sharpen the scheme and make a nice foil to the matte-finished, pale wood cabinets and white stone floor. A few dazzling touches, like the carved overhead rack hung with shiny copper pots, add more excitement and a distinctive French flair. The kitchen's generous size allows for plenty of storage in conventional base cabinets, but a separate pantry adds even more storage space and enhances the romantic, vintage look.

Right: *A mix of open and closed cabinets above a built-in, old-fashioned stove creates the effect of an oven niche. The enclosed cabinet conceals the range vent. An array of wooden rolling pins and a vintage spice cabinet are charming traditional touches.*

Right: *Lots of kitchens have a window above the sink, but few are as impressive as this one. Sunlight streams over the pine cabinets and island and reflects off the polished black granite countertops, enhancing the brightness of the space.*

Left: *Whitewashed walls, both stone and wood paneled, are a hallmark of fresh country style in any language. A generously scaled, white marble countertop is great for rolling out pastry dough or just tossing a salad.*
Below: *A special niche keeps this massive commercial stove out of the way and shows off its great looks, too. A stone base protects the wood floor from the commercial stove's exceptionally high heat. In front of the rustic, open shelving, a Windsor armchair, painted glossy black, echoes the room's smart black accents.*

BRIGHT PLANES OF COLOR—yellow, white, and black—balance the massive fire-engine-red stoves that take center stage in these striking kitchens. Even if your range isn't quite this impressive, the decorating principle is a good one: Several strong colors, used in the same intensity and cut with a large amount of white, are a fuss-free recipe for an exciting-looking kitchen. Of course, it doesn't hurt to have a few other things going on, like the big, white marble work counter in one of these kitchens, and the niche that encloses the stove in the other. Both kitchens share the rustic, cottage trait of displaying cooking tools and dishes on open shelves or hooks within easy reach of a busy cook or helpful guest.

Parlez-Vous Pretty?

HEART-STOPPING VISTAS of a winding river don't hurt, but this French country kitchen would be an inspiring beauty anywhere. Both pristinely clean and warmly charming, it's the epitome of chic—traditional-style. Bright white wood cabinetry with traditional raised paneling and furniture-style feet gets a sprightly touch with ball drawer and door pulls. White wood panels that match the cabinets downplay the fridge and dishwasher. A plain, contemporary picture window flanked by casement windows makes a simple frame for a gorgeous country view, and the black granite countertops add to the air of luxurious simplicity. A stainless-steel double sink and commercial-style range, plus a hard-working, good-looking oak floor, reflect the French sense of practicality that's as famous as its sense of style.

Below: *Chic checks in crisp blue and white look fresher than ever with their slightly wavy angles. A valance loaded with ripe vegetables adds color while complementing the blue-and-white patterned wallcovering. It's a combination of friendly patterns that's essentially French country.* ***Designer: Kimball Derrick, CKD, K. D. and Steele Cabinetry.***

Opposite, top: *A subtle foulard-style pattern on the tiled stove backsplash complements the other patterns in this kitchen. The warm wood of the range hood is echoed in the kitchen's handsome oak floor and traditional ceiling beams with corbel supports.* **Opposite, bottom left:** *Le breakfast bar, the higher level of a tiered island, has room for four Napoleon-style counter stools with pert bowed cushions that carry the theme. Diners can enjoy a chat with the chef and a great view, too.* **Opposite, bottom right:** *This elegant cabinetry is clean-lined, but it can't resist a few charming touches, like the arched Palladian-style glass cabinets over the work counter and the corner shelving with spindles. A pair of tall stacking cabinets adds pantry-size storage.* ***Cabinets: K. D. and Steele Cabinetry.***

A HEARTY FAMILY KITCHEN like this is just the thing for cooking up great spreads, concocting a few ethnic specialties, and hosting holiday parties. The ruddy stone tile floor makes a warm background for the rustic wood cabinetry that fills the space. Balancing these red-brown tones, an unusual olive-green ceiling with perimeter lighting and bright white counters and backsplashes bring in coolness and brightness. Counter stool cushions tie the color scheme together with fabric in tones of red, olive-green, brown, and white. The stainless-steel stove and fridge add more sparkle and modern flair, and the whole scene simmers with excitement. An important key to the welcoming ambience of this space is the spacious island that lets the cook stay close to snacking guests. Nearby, a built-in lighted china cabinet tops an informal bar. Guests can move comfortably from one area to another and enjoy every aspect of the space. Salud!

Opposite: *This kitchen's centerpiece is an overscaled island with a richly traditional paneled base and bright white stone top. It houses a prep sink and snacking space for four; the butcher-block section of the countertop provides plenty of work space, too.* ***Designer: Vicki Edwards, CKD, Kitchen & Bath Images.***

The whimsical hanging pot rack and rustic cabinets lend a country air, while the unique green-painted ceiling and commercial-style stainless-steel stove, backsplash, and range strike a modern, uptown note.

A Favorite Little Bistro

A beautifully crafted cherry range hood provides balance to the expansive stainless-steel backsplash. Pull-out racks for spices and oils are hidden behind narrow cherry-wood doors that flank the commercial-style range. ***Range: Viking.***

THE AMBIENCE of a much-loved crêperie is captured in this enchanting, bistro-inspired kitchen. The many wood touches lend a laid-back, homey feel, but the overall design is practical enough for even a professional cook. Functional touches include two full-size refrigerator/freezers and an innovative dishwasher with two drawers that allows the homeowner to use one for clean dish storage while filling up the second with used dishes. Other clever solutions include an array of cookbook shelves, glass-front pasta bins, and wine rack storage. A generously scaled island designed for informal dining offers a cherry unit on one end that's perfect for food prep and storage. Fine cherry paneling that runs around the soffit is a strong, unifying element. It's the perfect recipe for a warm, traditional look with up-to-the-minute commercial features.

Right: *This practical island combines a granite-topped section that houses a sink and breakfast bar with a butcher-block-topped section for food preparation. The built-in wine rack adds a charming touch.* ***Designer: Andrea Leshay, Design for Sale, Inc.***

Corner windows topped with discreet, natural-toned Roman shades make a fine focal point for this area of the kitchen. Flanking the windows, a pair of cherry cabinets with sliding glass doors shows off the homeowner's glassware and porcelain. Back-splash tiles that look like small stone bricks are a beguiling yet practical touch.

Italian Villa

A SPACIOUS, LUXURIOUS HOME deserves a kitchen to match, and Italian villa style provides the royal treatment. Inspired by the palatial yet airy homes of aristocrats from ancient times to the Renaissance, this style is sophisticated and luxurious but never heavy-handed. To create a masterpiece, start with an impressive shell: Specify tall, graceful Palladian

windows; generously scaled, arched doorways; and high ceilings. Continue with other grand architectural gestures, including ornately carved kitchen islands with marble insets for pastry-making, special knife racks, and lots of display space, both closed and open. Select formal, traditionally styled cabinetry in fine-grained hardwoods, either midtoned or in pale bisque finished tones, embellished with ornate, antiqued brass cabinet hardware.

Italy is one of the world's finest sources of quarried stone and artisan-made tiles, so your Italian villa kitchen is the perfect place for luxurious natural stone flooring, countertops, backsplashes, and even entire walls. You can choose opulent polished marble (sealed to resist stains); durable, dramatic granite; or subtly elegant tumbled marble—all work beautifully. Other practical luxuries: hand-painted Italian tiles to carry out your color scheme and decorating theme; serious wine storage racks; and a comfortable, handsome dining table and chairs.

Italian villa colors are the handsome neutrals of stone and wood mingled with the rich tones of oxblood, hunter-green, eggplant, and warm gold. Call on faux-finishing artists to conjure up the richly antiqued look of an ancient palazzo with richly dimensional sponged or frescoed plaster wall treatments. Accent with faux-bois woodwork finishes, and if you've always yearned for a bit of opulent gilding, feel free to indulge your Midas touch here. For the crowning effect, commission a custom mural depicting the Tuscan countryside, a Pompeiian vista, or a Renaissance still life à la Della Robbia. With an Italian villa kitchen, you're living "la dolce vita"—the sweet life.

Elegance Set in Stone

Below: *A magnificent stone vent hood and a backsplash made of oversize stone tiles create a quietly opulent focal point. Mottled granite countertops and cabinets with traditional raised panels are elegant and timeless.* ***Designer: Lila Levinson, ASID, CKD, CID, Accent On Design.***

THE KITCHEN of an Italian villa has always been an intriguing mix of the homespun and the opulent. Today's interpretation is lavish but appreciates the simple and practical. In the first kitchen, a classically proportioned range hood above an unobtrusive, drop-in cooktop is just one of the elements that evokes the spirit of this beguiling style. The plain wood plank floor, softened with the unexpected touch of an Oriental rug, also expresses the mix. Opposite the cooktop, a granite-topped table with open shelves and traditional Italian baskets offers extra storage. In the second kitchen, ceiling beams recycled from an old barn, a backsplash with the look of ancient stone, a knotty pine island with a freestanding furniture look, and a mix of wood and ceramic tile countertops contribute to the rustic yet gracious air. The ceiling beams make it easy to hang baskets and bunches of dried herbs and flowers.

Right: *The plaster range hood above the commercial-style stove was faux-painted to achieve the look of stone. Overhead, the baskets and dried flowers are traditional country accents—no matter what the country.* ***Designer: Diane Gassman, Interior Dimensions. Gas range: Dynasty; range hood: Vent-A-Hood.***

VIKING

Luxurious Classicism

Traditional cabinets with an antiqued oyster-white finish and subtle black detailing are the stars of this elegant Italianate kitchen. Marbled walls, an abundance of Italian marble, and ceramic tiles underscore the regal look. **Cabinets: Canac Kitchens.**

THE OPULENT but surprisingly subtle hallmarks of Italian villa style are clearly evident in these timeless kitchens. The color scheme, composed of subdued yet rich taupe and ivory tones accented in ebony, is very livable. The two kitchens shown here feature handsome natural flooring: One has marble tiles with black diamonds, the other uses wood. And both have furniture-quality cabinetry with lavish traditional detailing. Perimeter cabinets, islands, and other storage sections mix nicely with actual furniture pieces. The result: the look of a kitchen that's evolved over many decades, each era adding pieces that succeeding generations can value as antiques. A glimpse into adjoining rooms shows just how compatibly formal these kitchens are without sacrificing a bit of their high performance.

Opposite: *A large, elaborately carved range hood and tumbled-marble backsplash make a perfect frame for the oversize commercial-style range. An equally impressive cabinet with turned legs, deeply paneled drawers, and a granite top abuts the island. A coffered ceiling adds great drama overhead.* **Designer: Elizabeth Firebaugh, CKD, and David Snyder, Signature Kitchens, Inc. Cabinets: Canac Kitchens.** **Right:** *A long, two-tiered counter with a faux-marble finish borders the work area in this quietly opulent kitchen. The lower tier holds the sink and work counter; the upper offers plenty of elbow room for snacking guests.*

Richly Embellished

Below: *Decorative carving and a variety of open, closed, and glass-door storage areas on upper and base cabinets create a great-looking wall unit. The effect is that of an old-fashioned, freestanding china hutch, only much more spacious.* ***Designer: Betsey Meyer, CKD, CBD, Betsey Meyer Associates. Cabinets: Heritage Custom Kitchens.***

SURPRISINGLY COZY for a room with so many lavish details, this kitchen is made for entertaining family and friends on a regular basis. A soothing palette of browns and greens makes the room as comfortable as it is luxurious. Backsplash tiles of varying sizes and assorted green hues, from chartreuse to mint, run the length of the kitchen. A decoratively painted range hood adds a flourish of color that's echoed in the swagged window valance. Also setting the scene are a terra-cotta floor in naturally variegated tones, custom-stained cabinets, and granite countertops with beige and brown striations that pick up the color of the cabinets. On the other side of the room, a run of elaborately carved wall cupboards hangs above base cabinets with more pretty, carved detail. A sink next to the stove and another on the china cabinet's countertop add extra convenience. The full-size fridge is stationed next to the microwave, creating a second work station.

Right: *The centerpiece of the kitchen, this magnificent island is feature-packed with a wine cooler, warming drawer, under-counter fridge, and seating for four.*

PAINTED CABINETS in dark jewel tones are most often associated with American colonial or Scandinavian styles, but in today's freewheeling design environment, they work just as well to create a handsome, Italian-inspired space. In this kitchen, teal-green mixes nicely with natural-toned cabinets, black granite counters, and pale marble floors. The combination of painted and wood cabinets, a traditional look enjoying a current vogue, goes a long way in making it appear as though the kitchen has evolved gradually over time. Within the mix, high-performance modern appliances, including a commercial-style range, fit right in. Small, special touches contribute to this effect: vintage Italian pottery and jars that once held wine or oil, small paintings spotted unexpectedly here and there, an herb topiary, even a small Oriental rug. Personal finds like these make an appealing design statement and create a one-of-a-kind kitchen, which is just what the homeowners wanted.

Opposite: *A teal-green island with natural rush counter stools gives this kitchen a distinctive look. On the far wall, a classic wood cabinet houses an old-fashioned plate rack and spice drawers plus a built-in microwave, mixing traditional flair and modern convenience.* ***Kitchen designer: Pamela Goldstein Sanchez, CKD, CBD, Rutt of Atlanta. Interior designer: William C. Tidmore, ASID, and Robert A. Henry, ASID, Tidmore-Henry & Associates. Cabinets: Rutt of Atlanta.***

Above: *A sun country kitchen looks unexpectedly cool with a mix of sophisticated teal-green and natural-finish cabinets, richly detailed with bas-relief columns, curves, and other traditional detailing. Black granite countertops are a luxurious and practical choice.*

Left: *A high, beamed ceiling and a marble floor give this kitchen the look of a great hall of the past. Recessed lights throughout provide effective and up-to-date task lights. Take note of the paneled wood range hood, banded in tile that echoes the tile pattern on the stove backsplash.*

A Fairy Tale Come True

NOT CONTENT with castles in the air, these homeowners made their dream real in this irrepressibly romantic, elegantly crafted kitchen. Two classic finishes, antique-white and dark cherry, are used on traditionally carved cabinets to give a historical feeling and create balance. A complementary color scheme of fondant-pink walls offset by acid-green swagged window valances creates a freshness that coordinates nicely with other greens and the many touches of copper throughout the room. Like the color scheme, many lighthearted touches make this room livable as well as elegant. The 18th-century-style cherry island has an heirloom presence, and the top, though made of opulent granite, is round—the emblem of friendly dining. Wine racks, metal garden chairs, and a curvy chandelier enhance the marvelously romantic, elegant ambience.

Opposite: *Everything about this room is fit for royalty, but with a lighthearted touch. Fine antique-white cabinetry is freshened by fondant-pink walls. An impressive, 18th-century-style island in cherry with brass Chippendale-style pulls is eased with a friendly, round granite top and curvy bistro chairs.* **Right:** *A sink alcove under a pretty, arched pelmet frames the view and offers extra storage space. The mix of dark and antique-white cabinets gives this kitchen the look of a room that has evolved over generations. Faux-stone quoins at the doorway recall medieval castle walls.*

Mediterranean

SOUTHERN FRANCE, Italy, Greece, Spain, and Portugal are home to many of the world's most wonderful regional foods and wines, which may be why Mediterranean style is an inspired choice for the kitchen. Whether or not you make your own pasta or risotto, you'll be drawn to the designs of these warmhearted cultures. Where else could you find such richly creative elements that are both freshly inventive and historically honored? What's more, Mediterranean is hearty and practical, maximizing the simple pleasures of the rustic life.

To get the look, choose cabinets in oak or pine (or, for a bit more refinement, pecan or another distinctive wood) with wrought-iron or antiqued brass hardware. Display hand-painted pottery finds on a few simple open shelves, and use closed cabinets for serious storage. For countertops that are beautiful as well as

practical, you can't do better than the ceramic tiles for which Italy, Spain, and Portugal are world-famous. Choose your color scheme—rich royal-blue, sun-yellow, and white is an especially beloved trio—and go a little wild, with bright, bold tiles on countertops and backsplashes. Feel free to indulge in a bril-

liantly colored edging and even a custom-designed tile mural for over the stove. On walls, try the eye-catching combination of heavily textured plaster or stucco walls inset here and there with a jewel of a ceramic tile. For kitchen dining, find a wood table with a distressed finish to pair with rustic chairs in wood or in wood and leather with brass nail-head trim. Accessorize with a wrought-iron pot rack, hanging garlic braids or colorful dried peppers, and herbs in terra-cotta pots for a look that's cheerful, bold, and timeless.

Dark and Handsome

Below: *The work island with deeply carved panels has the look of a major piece of freestanding furniture. Above the work island, an ornamental iron pot rack hung with a wealth of copper cookware steals the show.*

WHETHER THE PRIMARY influence is Italian, Spanish, Portuguese, or Greek, Mediterranean style always includes an abundance of beautiful tile work. Most often, it's a tile floor and elaborately designed tile backsplash. This dramatic kitchen has these elements, but it also boasts an unusual tiled ceiling set between polished, exposed ceiling beams. Tile appears again in a lively spiral-motif design around the handsome double windows. Black wrought-iron and grandly scaled wood furniture are also hallmarks of Mediterranean style, and this kitchen makes good use of these signature pieces. A dramatically carved island with a bounty of copper pots hanging overhead is an unbeatable focal point that would work in almost any style kitchen. Beyond the island, a cooking alcove enclosing a commercial-style stove has practical, great-looking tiled walls and an arched doorway with elaborate wood molding. Creating a soothing background for it all, white stucco walls add subtle textural interest.

Opposite: *A stainless commercial-style refrigerator/freezer/cooler unit with a see-through door is built into a stuccoed wall; on the perpendicular wall, an interesting stepped stack of shelves is incised into the stucco for a truly unique look.*

Pastry
2c flour
butter

Glowing Glamour

"GLAMOUR" ISN'T USUALLY a word associated with kitchens, but in this case, it fits. Spectacular but not overdone, this kitchen is filled with masterful touches to delight the eye. The overall golden glow is simply enchanting. Antique-white and white-glazed wood tones, earthtone granite, and white marble all blend in a soft, sophisticated scheme. Antiqued terra-cotta tiles in an interesting mix of neutral tones contribute to the earthy effect. Lavish bas-relief carvings on the range hood and selected cabinets are more visual treats. Instead of the usual upper cabinets, a wall of windows lets the light in, contributing to the sunny Mediterranean-garden feeling. Balancing the clean, nature-loving design, opulent touches like the pretty iron-and-crystal chandelier over the simple dining table and coordinating wall sconces between the windows create a sense of occasion.

Below: *A mix of antique-white and honey-toned wood rubbed with a white overglaze makes for beguiling cabinets and a fabulous range hood cornice. Perimeter countertops in white marble echo the elegant pale tones.* ***Designer: Anita Brooks, ASID, Ultimate Kitchens.***

Left: *Mottled earthtone granite on the sink island is repeated in a cutout on the stove backsplash. Beyond the central island, unadorned modern windows (rather than the more typical Mediterranean Palladian windows) let in floods of light above a second sink.*

A Bountiful Buffet

SOME KITCHENS are made for hospitality, and this is one of them. There's plenty of room for food preparation, stylish storage, comfortable service, and, best of all, mingling. In this kitchen, two, three, or more cooks can easily work side by side and back to back. Striking black countertops are long enough to handle active food prep at one end and festive buffet service at the other. At the end of the work corridor, a bright commercial-style stainless-steel stove and range hood stand out even more thanks to a classic mural backsplash. Another unique focal point is the trompe l'oeil wall that depicts faux brick and ancient columns twined with vines. An oversize pot rack above and ruddy terra-cotta tiles below set the stage for a most hospitable kitchen and many memorable feasts.

Above: *Black countertops and colorful tile backsplashes and borders make a dramatic contrast that's a big part of this kitchen's lively style. Simply designed pale wood cabinets add soothing balance; black cupboard door pulls relate the cabinets to the countertops.* ***Designer: Jim Dove, Canterbury Design, Kitchen Interiors.*** **Far Right:** *Here, an impressive custom china cabinet stands sentry. A glass-front cabinet flanked by open shelves shows off a treasure trove of colorful pottery and ceramics. Below, an array of cubicles in a unique starburst shape store wine in great style. A surrounding trompe l'oeil wall painting of bricks and vines is a signature touch.*

Above: *A chic stainless-steel stove and range hood are surrounded by a variety of handsome tiles. Mini-tiles in an earthy solid color are bordered with fruit-motif tiles along the perimeter counters; larger tiles in a classic pedestal fruit bowl mosaic make a handsome backsplash.*

An extra-long kitchen island runs the length of the room, providing ample room to stage just about any social event these homeowners could cook up. A parallel counter provides the same amount of work surface again, so the area is perfect for two cooks or more.

A Perfect Balance

OFF-WHITE CABINETRY makes a handsome background to rich earthtones in this rustic but elegant Mediterranean kitchen. The black, brass-accented stove, two generously sized dark wood cabinet units, and a beautifully polished wood island balance the white beaded ceiling and antique-white cabinets with subtle black detailing. Upper cabinets with curved tops and leaded glass doors evoke a romantic old European air. A stone tile floor in a warm mix of earthy red, gray-green, brown, taupe, and ivory carries a more important design role than in most kitchens, adding a subtle pattern. Granite counters, highly polished on top, are left roughly cut on the edges—an intriguing mix that echoes the spirit of this distinctive room.

Left: *Dark wood cabinets with the look of antique bureaus on the interior perimeter wall and a handsome granite-topped island in the same dark wood add presence as well as plenty of extra work space.* **Right:** *An antique-white cabinet with black accents and a black granite counter has the appearance of a freestanding china cabinet/breakfront, thanks to a beaded-wood back panel and a pair of curved supports bridging the upper and lower cabinets.* ***Designer: Kimball Derrick, CKD, K. D. and Steele Cabinetry.***

LIKE NEIGHBORING Spain and Italy, Portugal justly claims artistry in ceramic tile among the elements that have enticed homeowners for centuries. In this warm-hearted kitchen, tiles in a great array of patterns make a spectacular backsplash. Interestingly, these tiles are in the sedate color scheme of cobalt-blue and white, a combination loved the world over. Unlike some of the more vivid color schemes typically seen, this one never intrudes, tires, or goes out of style. Thick white stucco walls, a big, brass-embellished stove, and terra-cotta floor tiles contribute to the Mediterranean-style room. A long table of rustic wood, highly polished, offers plenty of room to host family and friends. Copper cookpots, terra-cotta pots of herbs, fresh garlic braids, and the characteristic glassware of the region complete the spirited look. It may be simple, but it's anything but plain.

Blue-and-white ceramic tiles make a beguiling backsplash for this unusual sink hewn out of stone. Above, a stuccoed shelf holds glassware with blue- and green-tinted edges, a characteristic of handmade Mediterranean pieces.

Opposite: *The heavy, stucco-beamed doorway lintel and overhead beams exude Mediterranean style; a sprightly wrought-iron chandelier is the perfect finishing touch.*

Right: *The enameled, brass-accented stove takes center stage, its lively tile backsplash the perfect place to hang cooking utensils at hand's reach. Thick windowsills echo the heavy, stuccoed range hood that acts as an extra shelf for cookpots.*

Echoes of the Past

LIKE A WONDERFUL Renaissance painting, this room resonates with a sense of history. So artfully are all elements put together, it's difficult to isolate exactly what gives the room its wonderful ambience. Mellow tones prevail, casting all in a soft light. Honeyed and darkly elegant wood tones work in concert to create a sense of a room that has evolved through the generations. Every touch is right, thanks to careful research: The mellow burgundy-colored window wall is as familiar as a favorite oil painting. The heavily carved dark wood table/island and range hood decoration also add to the ambience. In deft counterpoint to the beautiful cabinets and carvings, rustic baskets and pottery, plain copper pieces, and a very personal mélange of informally propped artwork cast their spell.

Left: *A kitchen island along the lines of a sofa table is an elegant solution that also offers plenty of work surface and extra storage space below. A drop-in cooktop and wall oven are subtly introduced to the space, and the range hood is a work of art with Della Robbia–style carvings echoed on the island.*

Right: *Honey-toned cabinetry and darker wood on the island and range hood share beautifully scaled, opulent carvings in Renaissance style that recall Della Robbia garlands of fruit and greenery.* ***Cabinets: Wood-Mode.***

Designed for a Crowd

A tumbled-marble backsplash and pretty cabinetry with subtle decorative accents create a romantic, provincial look. A double sink, built-in microwave, drop-in cooktop, and double wall oven pack in practicality. ***Oven and cooktop: Thermador; microwave: GE; sink: Kohler; faucet: Grohe.***

AN OLD KITCHEN, laundry room, and powder room were reconfigured and redesigned to create this splendid kitchen. The room's cool yet welcoming air owes a lot to luxury materials used with restraint. The combination of alabaster-white traditional cabinetry with provincial French decorative accents and pale limestone tile flooring visually expands the space, but the design goes even further. In a pale kitchen like this, dark accents are important to provide balance. To achieve this goal, dark green granite countertops and a fabulously carved dark wood island are used to good effect. Beyond the kitchen's work area, against a newly constructed wall, a stately wall unit with solid wood base cabinets and glass-door upper cabinets stores extra serveware and shows off a fine porcelain collection. These cabinets are out of the way but express the same spirit as the rest of the kitchen.

Left: *Made from an antique fireplace mantel, this spectacular sink island, with lion's head columns and an ogee-edged top, steals the scene.*

Right: *A significant part of this kitchen's charm is the traditional cabinetry enriched with scalloped, arched recessed panels or applied carved decorations. The white cabinets coupled with pale limestone flooring make this spacious kitchen seem even roomier.* ***Designer: Barbara Facetti, Custom Kitchens, Inc. Cabinets: Heritage Custom Kitchens.***

Columns That Add Up

ALTHOUGH THE WORD "classic" is loosely used to mean "traditional," real classical style originated in ancient Greece, and its hallmarks have been reborn in neoclassical eras ever since. In this kitchen, neoclassical style returns to its rustic, Mediterranean roots. The result is dignified but also spacious and earthy. White reeded columns rising to the ceiling make an impressive divider between the work island and small desk as well as act as the focal point of the entire kitchen, inspiring thoughts of splendor and majesty. It's details like this that make a kitchen, filled with modern innovations but inspired by the past, look like a coherent whole. Adding to the warm atmosphere, the tile floor, a mix of earthy greens and browns, and the dramatic, dark backsplash work together to balance the pale cabinets. It's easy to imagine this room welcoming family and friends as well as large parties.

Left: *A pair of ceiling-height, classically reeded columns separates the work island from a small, granite-topped desk, adding visual drama to the space. The lines of the columns echo the vertical casement windows and help tie the elements of the room together.*

Right: *Modern appliances blend in with the traditional feel of the room by way of traditionally paneled, bisque-finished cabinet facades. Cabinets running all the way to the ceiling continue the vertical look created by the columns.*

Dishing up Some Favorites

In the dining area, a built-in run of lower cabinets includes fittings for a computer, while a row of upper cabinets shows off pots, bowls, and other tabletop treasures.

When you have a special collection that's especially appropriate for displaying in a kitchen or dining room, you can go beyond the usual china hutch or curio cabinet, as this homeowner did. Deep, white crown moldings, mounted at soffit height, have a classically formal air, but when used as a practical plate rail, they're simply ingenious. The color scheme is a classic, too: The mix of creamy walls and white woodwork is a traditional favorite for its ability to create a sense of depth. Cabinets in antique olive-green are mixed in with warm, natural-finished cabinets to give the look of a room in which heirloom pieces have been assembled over time. In addition to state-of-the-art appliances and ample counter and storage space, this kitchen includes thoughtful touches that make the room work even better.

Antique-looking cabinets house the high-performance oven in style. Above the sink, traditional wall racks make putting away dishes easy and add to the plate-happy design theme.

The homeowners' collection of colorful, one-of-a-kind plates gets the attention it deserves perched on deep, soffit-height moldings that act as plate racks. Creamy wall paint contrasts subtly with white molding and other trim to create depth, while antique-green and natural-toned cabinets add rustic charm. **Designer: McDonald & Moore Ltd.**

The Touch of the Artisan

Some Mediterranean-style kitchens seem born for a rustic cottage, while others are elegant enough for a villa. But they all share one distinctive quality: the charm of elements handcrafted by artisans and artists. In these three kitchens, such touches abound. In one, a cavernlike space has an air of romance accented by ribbons of blue-and-white tile. In another, charming yet practical design elements include cabinetry with pretty, old-fashioned plate racks and an inventive, three-tiered island. In the same kitchen, an elegant white-on-white tiled backsplash depicts a fruit and bread basket, the material and look similar to popular Italian ceramicware. In the third kitchen, a counter-high fireplace with a Gothic-inspired surround of diamond-shape terra-cotta tiles provides a beautiful focal point. However it's achieved, the look is warm, creative, and inviting.

Opposite: *A rustic, almost cavernlike dining spot evokes the cool hillside cottages of southern Europe. Intricate blue-and-white tile patterns around the doorway and a treasure trove of silver on the small table add a bit of whimsy and brightness to balance out the primitive atmosphere.*

Above: *A ceiling of heavy but finely finished beams, romantic provincial furniture, and a handsome fireplace surround of terra-cotta tiles set in a diamond pattern make this eat-in kitchen an inviting place.* **Designer: Scott Seibold, Canterbury Design Kitchen Interiors.**

Left: *Rich cream-colored cabinetry is embellished with bas-relief columns, rope borders, raised panels, and other charming details. The central island, an unusual design with a black marble top for display, a white ceramic tile top as a bar sink surround, and a butcher-block top for food prep, is a practical and witty stand-out.* **Designer: Scott Seibold, Canterbury Design Kitchen Interiors.**

Retro Kitsch

WHAT'LL IT BE, sweetie? How about the fun, funky, confident style of a diner? You know, that bright, brash look from the 1930s to '50s, when America took to the road and "fast food" meant a slice of homemade pie with your burger. This practical style emphasizes easy cleanability with smooth, glossy surfaces wherever possible, but it's also youthfully exuberant and unashamedly fun. If this look speaks to you, pull a few bright primary colors and hot pastels together: Try red, turquoise, and yellow, or coral-pink, mint-green, and royal-blue. Add lots of bright white and a pinch or two of black for drama. The classic retro kitchen features white cabinets—either in high-gloss painted wood or, for the adventurous, metal finished with appliance-grade paint. Finish with lots of shiny chrome counter edging and cabinet hardware, and mix with classic white, chrome, and stainless-steel appliances, large and small. (Some of the best retro designs, from blenders and phones to pudgy chrome toasters, have recently become available again, combining fun old profiles with today's high performance.)

Blend in retro-patterned vinyl or linoleum flooring and laminate countertops, and order a chrome-and-vinyl dinette or snack counter on the side. Garnish with perky café curtains (only on windows that aren't near the stove) or a fabric valance in '40s-inspired patterns over metal Venetian blinds. Seek out retro-print fabrics (available new or at flea markets). A retro kitchen is the perfect place to showcase collectibles like pink Depression glass or trademarked Fiestaware. If your taste secretly runs to more kitschy collectibles, such as soft drink bottles, themed salt-and-pepper shakers, or old road signs, they'll be right at home here, too. Be sure you include some glass-front cabinets or extra wall shelves, painted glossy white, to show off these prized possessions. As a final touch, why not hang a blackboard to announce today's specials or, for a more practical use, to record phone messages? Whether you're in a slick urban space or a suburban house, retro kitsch style serves up comfort with fun.

A Fresh, Cool Chic

Above: *An adjacent dining area continues the stylish color scheme and retro feel of the kitchen. The large checkerboard pattern on the wall helps incorporate the "diner" feel, while the chrome floor lamp speaks of times gone by.*

RETRO STYLE can be playful and funky, but it can also be sophisticated, as in this kitchen that recalls the urban chic of Paris in the '30s. What makes the look so sharp? First, there's the color combination: Lettuce-green, white, and black make a snappy color scheme that works in the adjacent room as well as in the kitchen. Then there's the intriguing mix of vintage and modern appliances. The white cabinets topped with black granite do a great job of uniting the old-time footed cast-iron sink with the modern stainless-steel range. Here's the place to accumulate your flea market or antique shop finds. Look for thick, white restaurant china, small chrome appliances from the 1920s through the '40s, old silver flatware in art deco patterns—the works. Finish off with black-and-white photos of prewar urban scenes, and voilà! You'll always have Paris!

Left: *A bar sink with exposed plumbing is set into a small counter that adds a bit of extra space for a vintage-style, chrome toaster. Clever planning makes room for a small marble dining table paired with vintage-style side chairs painted shiny black.*

Right: *Old and new fixtures and appliances can look great together if they're bridged by cabinetry that incorporates the colors of both. Here, white cabinets with granite counters do the trick.*

Pastels With Punch

THESE KITCHENS are a throwback to the 1930s, '40s, and '50s. They demonstrate why so many people are taking to retro style in the kitchen, the place where so many childhood memories are created. For some people, retro's charm is its distinctly tongue-in-cheek approach to "space-age" design. For others, this kind of decor offers all the pleasures of nostalgic styles, but without the ruffles. In one kitchen, yellow-green metal cabinets sparked with lots of chrome are surprisingly easy on the eyes. A vintage stove and fridge—in white, of course—keep company with glass-front cabinets with rounded corners and, again, more chrome than a '57 Chevy. In the other, a sky-blue stove and matching laminate countertops go nice as pie with white cupboards and a multicolored ceramic-tile snack table. Colorful collectible pitchers, salt-and-pepper shakers, and other dining memorabilia give the room a playful picnic air.

Below: *As much fun as a playroom, this retro kitchen relies on a shade of sky-blue popular in '50s convertibles, a sprinkling of other paintbox colors, and a lot of clean, clear white. Since all the colors are the same intensity, the effect isn't jarring, just lively.*

Opposite: *Tangy yellow-green is an offbeat but sophisticated color for this cool retro kitchen. A bold black-and-white checked floor ties in with the silvery look of chrome and the bright white of vintage appliances.*

Collectible soft drink signs and whimsical accessories of all kinds, some useful, some just fun, crowd the walls and hang from the ceiling. Storage cabinets and shelves keep grocery items out of sight and clutter under control—an important factor when the look depends on displaying a lot of collectibles in a relatively small space.

America's Golden Age, a period usually defined as the Gay 1890s to the early 1900s, is a great era to reproduce in today's retro kitchens. The period's optimistic mood and fascination with "modern" inventions work together to create a hospitable, fun environment. In one kitchen, a splendid ruby-red refrigerator and commercial-size range take center stage. Its 1890s style bursts with nostalgic appeal, and the stimulating crimson-and-daffodil-yellow color scheme is exciting and cozy at the same time. Yellow floral swagged draperies, lavishly fringed in red, add a formal feeling and help balance the massive red appliances. The other kitchen pulls out all the stops in a red-and-white scheme that recalls an early-1900s sweets shop. The cozy, welcoming feeling is best expressed in the watermelon-motif bistro chairs and heart-shaped accessories. A vintage-style stove is an important part of this nostalgic setting, and its black color anchors the scheme.

Opposite: *Ruby-red appliances are undeniably the centerpiece of this retro kitchen. Key to keeping this color scheme under control is to limit the number of hues you use. Here, the scheme is confined to red, yellow, and neutrals such as chrome and wood.*

Heartland

BREAD

A DELIGHTFUL SENSE of fun animates this retro-style galley kitchen, all tricked out in a surprising but successful color scheme that combines pink and white with spicy red, yellow, and black accents. In a room that's short on space but long on style, a strong, unusual concept works best. Here, collectibles are key, from the red-handled kitchen utensils on the wall to the cartoon-figure fridge magnets and cookie jars that provide a whole new wacky take on the usual barnyard friends found in more conventional kitchens. A '50s-style fluorescent tube lamp is a small but important touch in creating the retro look, right from the top. Outside the working galley, an inviting bay-window area is the perfect spot for a '50s-themed dinette, complete with harvest-gold vinyl cushions and a tabletop jukebox.

Pert and pink, this retro range cooks up some fun in the decor department. Cookpots, canisters, and even the clock—all collectibles from the 1930s through '50s—help carry the look.

Opposite: *Black and white add snap in the shape of checkerboard flooring and striped curtains; pink-and-white cabinets are spiced up with cheery red-and-black metal pulls. A dizzying array of cartoon collectibles helps carry out the fun color scheme.*

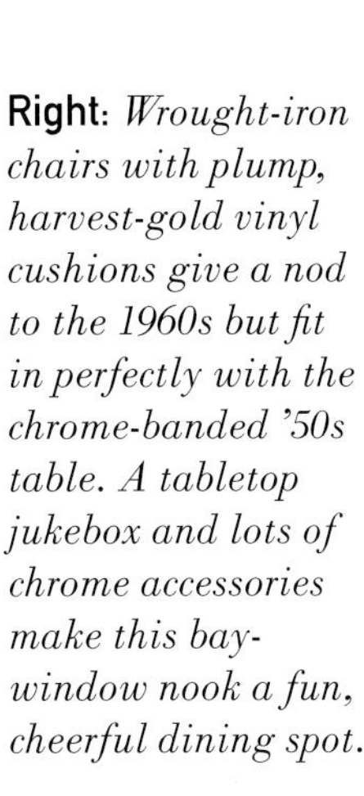

Right: *Wrought-iron chairs with plump, harvest-gold vinyl cushions give a nod to the 1960s but fit in perfectly with the chrome-banded '50s table. A tabletop jukebox and lots of chrome accessories make this bay-window nook a fun, cheerful dining spot.*

Sweet as Pie

Below: *Cobalt-blue has always been a classic choice to pair with white, and it looks as good as ever in this heartwarming space. A magnificent vintage stove, enameled in cobalt-blue, works perfectly with homespun checked curtains, distressed-finish chairs, and blue-banded ceramic mixing bowls.*

CHEERFUL AS A sunny day, these bright kitchens exude a friendly spirit that can be family-oriented or downright funky, depending on your perspective. The early 1900s offer plenty of nostalgic traditions to remember, back before superhighways made it easy to bypass small towns and their charms. One of these kitchens brings home the fun of an old-time family vacation or a Sunday afternoon social every day; the other evokes the appeal of a gingerbread-baking grandmother's kitchen. In one kitchen, a round table covered in a froth of white lace is the perfect companion to ice cream parlor chairs, and the vintage-style white stove fits right in. The roadside signs, fruit-patterned dishtowels, and even the Raggedy Ann 'n Andy hail mostly from the 1930s and '40s and contribute to the kitchen's whimsical, lighthearted air. In the other kitchen, white stars with cobalt-blue, most notably in the turn-of-the-century stove.

Opposite: *Before superhighways—let alone the Internet superhighway!—there were meandering roads that led past charming little eateries like those evoked by this fun kitchen. Ice cream shoppe sweetheart chairs, old signs, and well-chosen accessories all convey a nostalgic, but entertaining, space.*

TOURISTS ROOMS
LOCKWOOD-MAC DONALD
HOSPITAL
BEES
Royal
Crown
COLA

Rustic Lodge

GET AWAY from it all without leaving home, in a rustic lodge/cabin-style kitchen. How to create it? If you don't live in a log house, the next best thing is exposed wood beams and open rafters, exposed brick or rustic wood paneling on interior walls, and wide-planked wood floors. Then, go for cozy textiles to

provide creature comforts. Because rustic residences have existed in every culture since early times, the style influences available today are wonderfully rich and varied. For an American pioneer cabin feeling, decorate with colorful quilts, afghans, and rag rugs, plus leather-upholstered seating in traditional style with exposed wood. For a sophisticated ski lodge look, indulge in luxurious faux-fur rugs and contemporary leather seating. For a rustic look inspired by warmer climes, choose Southwestern style: a blend of colonial Spanish and Native American influences expressed in wrought-iron accessories, cool stucco or plaster walls, and serape-inspired fabrics in off-white, brick, blue, and yellow.

What works everywhere: a palette of earthtones—greens, browns, and tans, accented with autumn-leaf accents in terra-cotta, brick-red, and gold. Casual woods such as oak, with its pronounced grain, or knotty pine are right at home, and a mix of built-in and freestanding pieces helps complete the casual look. For countertops, choose butcher block, and add

extra workspace with a kitchen island that may simply be a hearty little table with lower shelves. For dining, look for an overscaled, solid wood dining table with rough-hewn chairs or even trestle benches. Keep window treatments simple: Use unadorned panes if privacy allows, or, at most, choose wood shutters or plain muslin Roman shades. Keep metals matte (pewter, not chrome; brushed-finish, not shiny stainless steel), and keep appliances under cover with matching wood-trim fronts. Then kick back and relax: In a kitchen this down to earth, forget cabin fever!

LOG HOMES don't have to be dark and low-ceilinged, as this airy kitchen shows. Balance between spaciousness and coziness, light and dark, rough and smooth, is the secret to this room's timeless appeal. A volume ceiling creates a lot of breathing room, while simple cabinets painted pale gray add a soothing, rather sophisticated touch. The minimalist setting is warmed by the strongly grained wood floor that visually links the upper and lower levels of the room. A sunny window nook with natural-finish wood walls creates a smaller version of the log cabin look, lightened up with a white-painted table and banquette. On the purely practical side, the kitchen provides the basics in style with no fluff: a range and range hood, sink with gooseneck faucet, and island with plenty of storage space for the homeowner's cooking utensils and books.

A cozy dining nook with natural-finish wood walls seats a crowd, thanks to a built-in banquette. A mix of rose, white, and wood-brown fabric cushions and pillows adds a romantic note that's in contrast with the area rug underfoot.

The Log Look Lightens Up

Opposite: *High-beam artistry juxtaposes rough-cut beams in a two-story ceiling with pale, painted wood cupboards below, for an effect that's almost sculptural. Interesting mixed-wood stools and strongly patterned Native American–motif area rugs bridge the rough and the smooth.*

Primitive Beauty

NONSYMMETRICAL, rough-hewn pieces of wood, beautifully polished, make an extraordinary kitchen. The cabinets, table, and chairs look as much like sculpture as they do kitchen furniture. Even the light fixture, made of simply hung sheets of wood, breaks the rules in an interesting way. The overall effect is organic and warm, rich in tactile and visual appeal. At the same time, it has a primitive, storybook-lodge feeling that makes it perfect for a getaway home. A hearty dining table offers plenty of room to seat eight on a collection of engagingly different chairs. A black stove keeps company with a breakfront cabinet that houses a second cooktop. Short lengths of narrow strip flooring in a variety of dark and light tones create a parquet look—yet one more note in this symphony of woods.

Left: *A rustic yet polished wall cabinet offers plenty of storage, including a row of practical cup hooks under the upper cabinets. Polished wood countertops, their edges randomly hewn, provide more work space and storage.*

Right: *It's easy to accommodate one more at this hospitable, extra-long table that's the centerpiece of this kitchen. Mismatched chairs add to the charm of the room, enhancing the sense that everything was handmade as it was needed over time.*

THIS LOG HOME pulls out all the stops in re-creating the look and spirit of a mountain lodge from a century ago—only much better. The kitchen, for one thing, is a marvel of modern conveniences in a relatively small space. Two dishwashers and two sinks, a commercial-style range, and a built-in microwave are housed in a space that's both soothing and dramatic. Bisecting the roomy island, a real tree trunk creates a look that's highly inventive but rustically faithful to the spirit of the house. The variegated wood floor, honey-toned cabinets, and coordinating terra-cotta tile countertops create a visual flow that expands the space. And that's just the work area! A two-story great room joins the more modestly scaled kitchen by way of a short flight of steps. Native American– and cowboy-themed fabrics and fine art inject a lively note and carry out the Old West feel.

Opposite: *A real tree trunk piercing this kitchen's island and ceiling acts as both a supporting beam and a conversation-starter. Topped with terra-cotta tile, the functional island houses a dishwasher, bar sink, and extra storage space.*

A great hall of vast proportions features a built-in eating counter adjoining the kitchen. Iron braces secure the impressive exposed-beam end wall; traditional log home construction gives the side walls a cozy feeling despite the room's size.

Wood-Loving Lodge Look

This kitchen features a double-wide commercial-style stove and range hood in scale with the room's imposing high-vaulted ceiling. A sink island provides an informal divider between the kitchen and adjoining family room. **Manufacturer: Rocky Mountain Log Homes.**

THREE KITCHENS illustrate three different ways to create the rustic appeal of the lodge look. In one, a high-vaulted ceiling uses a combination of side-by-side boards on the side walls and half-round chinked beams on the end walls. Softening the look are an antique farm table, a rawhide-shaded pendant lamp, and a rug depicting trout in a stream. In another, a low-beamed ceiling creates a cozy look. Adding to the kitchen's traditional log cabin charm are a fieldstone-based eating peninsula and casual window seat in the curtained bay window—a comfortable plus in any kitchen. The third kitchen looks more contemporary than the others by virtue of its simplicity. Clean and plain as a Swedish sauna, even the range hood is made of knotty pine. There's a log home for just about any taste, and these kitchens are just a sampling.

Right: *A dining peninsula with a fieldstone base and red ceramic-tile top combines the rustic beauty of natural materials with the cheerful effect of red. An array of traditional accessories adds to the room's cozy feel.* **Manufacturer: Rocky Mountain Log Homes.**

Left: *Virtually every surface is knotty pine wood in this warm, clean-lined kitchen, and all corners are rounded off for an extra user-friendly touch.* **Manufacturer: Honka Homes USA, Inc.**

LOST AT SEA
UNIVERSAL ATLAS
WONDERS of the WORLD
ALL AROUND THE WORLD COOKBOOK

Into the Woods

CONTEMPORARY STYLE isn't usually the first thing that comes to mind when the subject is log homes, but this savvy kitchen shows how compatible modern style and log construction can be. Modern design, which believes in showing materials and construction methods just as they are, takes to log home style with surprising ease. This special kitchen takes traditional log home elements like log beams and support columns and works them into a free-flowing modern space—without losing any of the warmth and solidity that make log homes appealing. Rounded countertops, ceilings, peeled support beams, and smoothly finished knotty pine surfaces add to the artful melding of nature and modernity.

Left: *A magnificent fieldstone fireplace with a curved, polished wood mantel and seating perch stands out as a work of art. Nearby, a curvy staircase continues the free-form play of wood.* ***Designer: Murray Arnott Design Ltd. Contractor: Jamieson Brothers Construction.***

Right: *White ceilings at several levels curve around the space, magnifying the natural light from the room's many large windows. A rounded-end island with roomy display shelves echoes the rounded, free-form curves of the ceiling above.*

Polished Rusticity

THIS BRIGHT BEAUTY, a large house with lots of great views, shows how sophisticated a log home can be. High ceilings; lots of glass doors and windows; and pale, polished wood surfaces showcase the home's love affair with natural wood—but without the rough edges of a traditional log cabin. A wealth of special touches enliven the neutral-colored space. In the center of the living area, between the working kitchen and dining area, an authentically styled adobe stove evokes Southwest style in a big way. A mix of colorful ceramic and terra-cotta tiles, all highly polished, adds spark to the predominantly wood-toned room. Above the kitchen island, a white wrought-iron pot rack with whimsical animal silhouettes keeps company with canister lights on exposed tracks. This mix of the structural and the ornamental is all part of the charm.

Right: *Pale, polished wood cabinets and flooring make an interesting counterpoint to the log walls and cross beams overhead. Traditional cabinets are topped with practical butcher block for an uninterrupted look.* ***Manufacturer: Rocky Mountain Log Homes.***

A Mexican-style adobe stove accented with pink and teal-green tiles makes a great-looking focal point in this kitchen. In a deft design touch, a band of pink and green tiles separates the terra-cotta tile floor from the adjacent wood floor.

Ample windows and glass doors flood the dining area with mountain sunlight. A glass-topped table adds an unexpectedly modern look, while underneath the table, small, colorfully glazed tiles create the effect of an area rug—a fresh touch in the glazed terra-cotta tile floor.

Southwest Savoir Faire

SPANISH AND OTHER Mediterranean influences abound in this Southwest-style kitchen. Only the exposed half-round beams in the ceiling and along the exterior wall give away the fact that this kitchen is in a log home. Overall, the look is bright and clean—clearly the space of a homeowner who enjoys cooking up a feast from old family recipes or exotic new ones, but always for feeding family and friends. What's key: Large expanses of white walls suggest stucco or adobe; rich cobalt-blue ceramic tiles add attractive accents traditional to the Southwest. White ceramic-tiled perimeter counters offer ample work space, and an angled work island provides even more. The big white refrigerator and microwave oven are free-standing, not enclosed in cabinetry as might be expected, for a look that's down to earth and informal. Traditional glass-shaded pendant lamps on bright brass chains add just the right amount of task lighting and a healthy dose of charm.

Left: *Handsome arched windows banded in cobalt-blue are a great-looking design element. The same rich blue is found in ceramic tiles bordering all the countertops.* ***Manufacturer: Rocky Mountain Log Homes.***

Fieldstones make a dramatic border to a rustic alcove in this kitchen. Against all this wood, white ceramic knobs and cobalt-blue tile borders are bright accents.

The counter's hearty fieldstone base punches the earthy look up to the max. A pair of carved wooden chairs with red leather seats and brass nail-head trim is a conversation piece on its own.

Sun Country Serenity

Sunflower-yellow and cobalt-blue ceramic tiles make a splendid focal point as well as a practical backsplash for an eye-catching blue-and-brass range. Adjacent wood counters are rough wood, but countertops are yellow tile on top, blue along the edges, for a fun, festive look.

BRIGHT AND WELCOMING, this kitchen balances the airiness of a sun-flooded, open floor plan with the timeless solidity of brick, stone, stucco, and wood construction materials. Hosts, guests, and family members can all enjoy this generously scaled space together. Golden-yellows and cobalt-blue make a splendid ceramic tile backsplash that's also a great focal point. The yellow tile brings out the golden tones of the knotty pine used for cabinets and exposed beams throughout the room. Generously proportioned, the kitchen's soaring ceiling is made even loftier by a giant, angled skylight. In addition to the show-stopping range and backsplash, the basic work area includes a pair of handsomely carved unmatched islands, one housing a second sink. Terra-cotta flooring is a sensible complement to the other timeless natural materials used in this handsome space.

Left: *A nearby fireplace adds a friendly, rustic touch to this work area. Aged terra-cotta flooring, beautifully carved wood work islands, and a view to the great outdoors make cooking a pleasure.*

Right: *A low, exposed beam supported by fieldstone columns defines the entry to the great room. Broad lintels over the doorways echo the strong, horizontal design created by the exposed ceiling beams.*

Traditional

If you're seeking a no-fail recipe for elegance, the choice is unquestionably traditional. Strictly speaking, "traditional" means simply "not modern," but in the United States it has come to mean a handsome, refined look that borrows elements from several historical American and English styles. Based on 18th-century designs that express consummate symmetry and grace, traditional includes Queen Anne, Sheraton, curvy Duncan Phyfe, and Chippendale styles from the golden age of furniture design. Your traditional setting may also include romantic influences, from French to English Victorian.

For a dignified traditional look, choose maple or cherry cabinetry with cathedral-topped, raised-panel doors and brass hardware. For a lighter look that invokes 18th-century Scandinavian court life or even an English gazebo, choose cabinets and freestanding pieces from the same periods but in antiqued white rather than dark wood, and add a special piece in a pretty color with painted embellishments. Select some cabinets with leaded-glass doors, or add a freestanding curio to show off antique porcelain and silver collections in style. Top your cabinets with real or faux marble and granite countertops. To keep your period look, rely on appliance depots with tambour doors and wood appliance panels that match the cabinets. Underfoot, choose hardwood strip flooring or classic tiles.

Here's the place for a brass bar sink, a handsome island, and other luxurious touches. An oval or round breakfast table in maple or cherry with pretty, 18th-century-style chairs is a hospitable choice. Away from the stove, formal wallcoverings and window treatments are perfect for your traditional kitchen, and they're especially handsome in muted jewel tones: old gold, blue-green, federal-blue, burgundy, ivory, and old rose. They're also lovely in cameo-pale tones of tea-rose pink, primrose-yellow, celadon-green, sky-blue, and white. Either way, you'll find that the pedigreed look of traditional style is gracious—and wonderfully timeless.

Hallmarks of Elegance

Graciousness and dignity are the gifts of a traditional room that draws from both 18th-century styles and the Arts and Crafts influence. What makes the room so remarkable is that, except for the appliances, everything in the room could serve as well in a drawing room or library. The cabinets are standouts: Rich, lustrous cherry-wood cabinets with subtle brass hardware have the look of fine furniture. They're used as wall-hung cabinets flanking the range, as well as in a spectacular glass-front china cabinet between the windows. Base cabinets with brass banker's drawer pulls provide a wealth of additional storage. Further enhancing the library look, a brick build-out suggesting a fireplace surround encloses the microwave oven and additional storage. Ruddy brick flooring, darkened slightly to suggest age, and several small Oriental-style rugs complete a look that will be just as elegant in 100 years as it is now.

Right: *A generous island with the look of a fine console table includes a Georgian-inspired faucet and open display shelves. Highly polished black granite countertops; a black range; and black, gold-lined shades on the brass ceiling lamps add even more depth and drama to the room.* **Left:** *A cherry china cabinet sits center stage between practical casement windows enlivened by the sparkle of leaded-glass transom panels.* ***Designer: Donna Martin and Jim Downs, The Downs Group. Architect: Francis Giblin, Summit Design Associates.***

Hospitality on a Grand Scale

BEAUTIFUL CHERRY CABINETS are a subtly opulent choice in this Federal-style kitchen, but that's just the beginning. The kitchen abounds in grand gestures carefully handled so that they create excitement without disrupting the well-bred demeanor of the room. The first thing that captures attention is the fireplace: the one focal point that nothing else can match. Then there's the finished, beamed ceiling, which showcases an unusual level of workmanship—even in a kitchen of this high quality. The countertops are also a stand-out: Instead of the expected granite, they're made of stainless steel with a brushed-nickel, pewterlike finish. The generously scaled dining peninsula is supported by a section of a massive white column; again, a surprising choice, but one that fits. Offsetting all this elegance, a rustic oak floor and cheery checked curtains add a casual, friendly accent.

Above: *A beautifully crafted mantle over a real wood-burning fireplace makes an irresistible focal point in this already spectacular kitchen. Flanked by a built-in desk and china hutch with the look of freestanding furniture, the fireplace not only looks impressive but contributes mightily to the welcoming, cozy atmosphere.*

Left: *A massive column supporting the end of this table peninsula is an impressive, unusual touch that works well with the room's other grand gestures, like the formal coffered, beamed ceiling. A pair of commercial-size refrigerators takes on the appearance of double drawing room doors, thanks to beautiful paneling.*

Stainless steel with a brushed-nickel finish is an extraordinary choice for countertop surfacing, but its soft gleam and easy-care qualities make it a smart one. The island houses a drop-in cooktop and a bar sink; the long counter under the window houses the main sink and dishwasher.

Gracious Living

A side-by-side fridge paneled in pale knotty pine is flanked by narrow china cabinets, balancing the mass of the refrigerator and helping it blend into the traditional setting. An Oriental-style throw rug adds a touch of color and warmth underfoot. **Cabinets: Heritage Custom Kitchens.**

THIS GENEROUSLY SIZED KITCHEN is elegant but also wonderfully down to earth, thanks to an unusual mix of materials. Naturally finished, knotty pine cabinets are definitely casual, but, embellished with pretty, French country carved details, they attain a dressier appeal. Hand-painted tiles depicting fruits and vegetables add an easygoing charm that offsets the impressive commercial-style stove and dark granite countertops. An angled island houses a built-in oven, microwave, and dishwasher and serves as an informal buffet. As in all the best kitchens, natural light is abundant, but just as important is the well-sited task lighting throughout the room. Recessed fixtures in the ceiling; in custom, suspended units; beneath upper cabinets; and under the range hood all contribute to the drama and livability of the space.

The modern look of a commercial-style range is softened by a pretty tile backsplash mural and a decoratively scalloped range hood. The simple addition of a narrow wall topped with a corbel creates the effect of an oven niche, although the range is flush with the cabinets.

Right: *A microwave is housed at the end of the distinctive island, surprising guests in its unusual but practical placement. Opposite, a wall of glass-front cabinets showcases a collection of porcelain.* **Designer: Lois Perry Kirk, Kitchens Unique, Inc., by Lois.**

Historic Home Revived

THE FEDERAL PERIOD boasted a number of craftsmen whose fine cabinet design and workmanship raised the work to the level of art. This quietly beautiful kitchen was designed to accommodate two cooks as well as a heavy flow of traffic throughout the room. The practical space pays homage to our founding fathers' sensibility with exquisitely crafted cabinetry in white and federal-blue. The stone tile floor, in a lovely range of muted blues, golds, and grays, adds more subtle richness underfoot. On the stove backsplash and range hood, a lyrical floral treatment made of custom-painted tiles is a lighthearted touch. A mix of white and black granite countertops further enlivens the setting. Examples of modern ingenuity include a variety of refrigeration units for food storage as well as warming drawers to free up oven space. Mr. Franklin would have approved.

Above: *Federal-blue cabinets with graceful, cathedral-style glass doors enclose a collection of fine glassware. Below the granite countertop, a pair of compact refrigeration drawer units puts cool where it's convenient.* ***Cabinets: Heritage Custom Kitchens; refrigeration units: Sub-Zero.***

Left: *A cabinet tower with slender, cathedral-style glass doors stands at the end of a granite-top sink island. Below, a pair of warming trays frees up space in the oven, opposite.* ***Designer: Lois Perry Kirk, Kitchens Unique, Inc., by Lois. Warming drawers: Thermador.***

Right: *A hand-painted tile backsplash and coordinating trim tiles around the wood-paneled range hood add a pretty touch to the handsomely restrained room.* ***Range: Viking.***

Arch of Triumph

Graceful archways above the kitchen's base cabinets transform the division between kitchen and dining room into a dramatic and elegant design element. ***Designer: Joe Webb and Dennis Meyer, K. D. and Steele Cabinetry. Architect: Jim Good, K. D. and Steele Cabinetry.***

WINE-RED, the most enticing of traditional colors, transforms the workaday walls of this kitchen into a dramatic design asset. The wall color brings out the warm red undertones of the cherry-wood cabinets and makes the decorative white ceiling and wall trim moldings fairly sparkle. Center stage in this room's elegant drama is the repeated arch motif that softens the squared-off shape of cabinets and appliances. A series of archways divides the kitchen from the dining room for a lavish effect that would be hard to create with any other architecture. On the kitchen side, the arched dividers hold narrow wall cabinets, ensuring that a kitchen this beautiful doesn't sacrifice storage one whit. Arched panels over the commercial-size range and flanking cabinets echo the elegant archways leading to the dining room. A decorative ceiling and a brass-embellished range hood are just two of many eye-catching elements in this kitchen.

Left: *Elegant cherry cabinetry creates a warm and elegant ambience, from the amply sized sink island to the airy upper cabinets glassed on both sides. Black granite countertops add to the polished effect throughout.* ***Designer: Kimball Derrick, CKD, K. D. and Steele Cabinetry.*** **Right:** *In keeping with the classically decorative ceiling, an exuberant brass lamp with a multitude of milk-glass shades puts this entertaining room in the spotlight. Imagine it during the holidays!*

Antebellum Elegance

As airy and elegant as a conservatory in an old Savannah mansion, this kitchen pays homage to the great outdoors in a very refined way. Straightforward, American traditional cabinetry with raised panels and wrought-iron pulls is given a lighthearted treatment with a pickled, bisque finish of thinned whitewash. Curvy, traditional French-inspired counter stools and dining chairs are a pretty complement to the cabinets. The green granite countertops add to the garden ambience, as does the oil painting (a touch not usually found in a kitchen) at one end of the work area. Overall, the design mingles the best of yesterday and today: Timeless, luxury materials are used to embellish features our ancestors never heard of, but which we don't want to do without, such as the snack counter set into the work island. With innovations like these, we can re-create the gracious hospitality of the past in a delightfully informal way.

Left: *A bank of windows over the sink counter and a lovely array of Palladian windows in the adjacent dining area wash this kitchen in sunlight year-round. The light cabinets and white paint amplify the spacious, airy mood.*

Right: *Traditional cabinetry with a pickled finish gives a fresh, romantic feeling to this massive island housing the drop-in cooktop and a second sink, as well as counter seating at one end.*

Festive and Spirited

A FINE BURGUNDY HUE on the ceiling is a fearless stroke that gives this kitchen much of its distinctive great looks. Beautiful cathedral-front cabinets in lustrous cherry wood are set off by the burgundy walls and slightly pink-tinged taupe granite countertops. The same taupe tone, plus oyster-white and crimson-red, show up in the opulently patterned wallcovering and Roman shade. Just as distinctive, every corner that can be turned with a curved cabinet has been. Curved cabinets look especially elegant and take up only the amount of space needed, with no sharp or wasted corners. A handsome ceiling fixture in period style makes a dramatic design statement against the dark red ceiling. Oriental-style area rugs in predominantly rosy tones look great over the timeless black-and-white tile floor. This festive kitchen is undeniably elegant, but it's also always ready for a party!

Right: *Lavish red-patterned fabric on the Roman shade gives the window, a natural focal point, even more attention. Coordinated wallpaper helps balance the ceiling's vibrant hue. This much pattern could easily overwhelm, but the edited color scheme keeps it nicely inbounds.* ***Designer: Randall Sisk, Kitchens by Kieweno.***

Mirrored backsplash walls add sparkle to this jewel-toned kitchen. The wood-paneled refrigerator and microwave inset into an upper cabinet provide first-class service without attracting attention.

Curved cabinets in fine cherry wood create a gently rounded profile that's more visually pleasing than ordinary rectangular cabinets, not to mention safer for cooks and kids on the run. The inset cooktop and under-cabinet oven fit in smoothly and unobtrusively.

Left: *Open and airy, this kitchen's bright looks owe a lot to the surprise of whitewashed wood floors. In this light-hearted setting, traditional dark cherry cabinets look even richer.* **Designer: Dee Hurst Funk, CKD, Kountry Kraft.**

Right: *Elaborately carved details, including grape clusters and garlands, ornament the refrigerator panel as well as many of the cabinets. A granite-top desk and multicompartment shelving unit above are clever touches.* **Cabinets: Kountry Kraft.**

Victorian Lite

Reassuringly formal but more sentimental than most traditional styles, Victorian design celebrates nature, domestic life, and emotional ties as few other styles do. No doubt that's why this style has attracted fans for more than 100 years. This charming kitchen handles Victorian style with a new, light touch. A bold decision to whitewash the wood floors results in a wonderfully clean, spacious look that lets the charm of detail really show. Instead of busy wallpaper, this kitchen confines floral garlands and grape clusters to cabinet carvings, the fabric on small chair cushions, a few hand-painted backsplash tiles, and carefully chosen accessories. This romantic treatment of nature is a Victorian hallmark—but without the dark, cluttered effect once associated with the period style. Up-to-date features include multiple work islands, a built-in wall oven and microwave, and a compact but efficient desk area. Clearly, breaking a few Victorian rules yields some appealing new options.

A pretty corner cabinet displaying treasured china combines a soft, whitewashed color, decorative carved accents, and a graceful shape.

Vividly Victorian

IN A HOME infused with the spirit of Victoriana, this handsome, hardworking kitchen admirably carries the theme. Two cooks can work comfortably in this space, which provides plenty of work surfaces and storage. What's more, the kitchen is universally accessible: The vanity-style maple cabinetry allows room for a wheelchair to be used in the space. Turned posts on the ends of the island and gingerbread-style valances are charming details that enrich the overall look of the room and help it fit in with the rest of the Victorian-style home. Period light fixtures in white opaque glass draw attention to the luxuriously high ceilings. Along with the sparkling white window trim, the fixtures set off the dark jewel tones of the room. The white trim is a simple but effective way to visually connect the kitchen to adjoining rooms.

Left: *Dark and rich, the red-brown color gives this elegant, traditional cabinetry a distinctly Victorian feeling. The custom drop-pendant cabinet door and drawer pulls bring out the sensibility of the late 1800s.* ***Designer: Diane L. Berndt, CKD, CBD. Cabinets: Wood-Mode; cabinet hardware: Horton Brasses; appliances: GE; sinks and faucets: Kohler.***

Right: *A furniture-style island with traditional turned legs is an understated centerpiece in this kitchen. Dark gray laminate countertops complement the linoleum tile flooring, a "modern" material developed in the Victorian era.*

World Beat

CULTURES HAVE BORROWED from one another in every era since civilization began. Today, with modern travel and a new respect for the unique riches of every culture, we welcome elements from many lands into our uniquely personal living spaces. The result is an exotic mix that is sophisticated, fresh, and very energizing.

To conjure up world beat style, start with a neutral foundation: textured white plaster or grasscloth walls and practical stone or terra-cotta flooring. Add dark, distressed-wood cabinetry topped in rustic stone or faux-stone counters, and consider the weathered luxury of tumbled marble for backsplashes. Bring in simple storage with open shelves of varying heights, and keep appliances in the background with matching woodtone cabinet fronts. For color schemes, take inspiration from native textiles. Choose paprika, ebony, ivory, spice-brown, and gold in bold chevron patterns to evoke the drama of Africa, or pick the jewel tones of paisleys from old Araby. Select regal Chinese red and green or softer celadon and peony-pink to create Asian elegance, and mix in hammered, enameled brass and brilliant sari hues from the bazaar.

For casual dining, find simple wood, cane, and rush-seated stools, benches, or chairs pulled up to a counter or round table in wood, perhaps with a tile-inset top. Build up the look with pottery or porcelains, wooden bowls and spoons, woven baskets, hammered metal trays, and other practical artifacts. To keep the mix attractive, be sure to balance the scale (visual weight) of pieces, and stick with a few high-impact decorative accessories. Motifs from the natural world—whimsical frogs, elegant herons, dignified elephants, and tropical flowers and foliage are appealing and speak to the ecological awareness of the world beat homeowner. For an interesting, edgy accent, don't overlook iconoclastic art pieces devised of recycled industrial products: a hallmark of inventive local cultures around the world. The look? Exotic, yet down to earth.

Streamlined Sophistication

NOT A STROKE is wasted in this minimalistic kitchen that conveys the height of cool, worldly style. Throughout the room, many looks peacefully coexist. The pale austerity of the room suggests a Japanese influence. The island, with its distinctive brushed-steel end piece and witty black-cushioned counter stools, has hints of inspiration from New York or perhaps Milan. Accessories, including wooden boxes and animal statuary from Asia and woven rattan trays from Africa, offer a balancing warmth and rusticity. A space like this has no room for error or whim; each piece is carefully planned for and selected in advance. The result is a room both tranquil and intellectually stimulating—a room where people are the center of attraction.

Right: *Pale, polished wood-strip flooring is in the same tonal family as the wood of the cabinets and the front of the island. Sandblasted whitewashed brick walls, through which the natural colors show through, add a subtly interesting texture.* **Left:** *Glass jars holding spices from the Middle East; hand-woven baskets from Africa; and frisky, hyper-modern counter stools in bright steel and black all blend together surprisingly well in the hands of a master designer with a fresh, international viewpoint. Neutral colors keep the scheme under control.* **Designer: Clodagh Design.**

Medieval Fantasy

THIS ARTFUL KITCHEN is filled with romantic allusions to European and Middle Eastern cultures, with minaret-topped cabinets; tiles with the effect of lattice-work floorcloths; an imposing, heavily carved stone stove surround that recalls a castle fireplace mantel; and a massive wood island, also heavily carved with classical embellishments. Freestanding furniture, including low cabinets with green marble tops, flank the stove, while the opposite wall is filled with Gothic-windowed wall cabinetry. Other kitchens may have an exotic flair, but few can be said to transport homeowners and guests to a time of legend, romance, and fantasy. This one does.

Left: *An elaborately carved stove surround worthy of a castle hearth is flanked by Moorish-inspired wall cabinets with minaret tops and quatrefoil insets. A stainless-steel stove and a pair of green marble-topped bureaulike cabinets round out the space.*

Right: *An antique Spanish chandelier hangs over a beautiful island, which features a granite top and a heavily carved wood base that resembles a cathedral pew. Gothic-style mullions distinguish the glass fronts of these wall cabinets to carry out the medieval fantasy theme.*

Serene Balance

MINIMALISTIC SPACES that might seem sparse if done Western-style often come across as serene when animated by an Eastern sensibility. As the American home becomes more of a retreat, and consumers expand their tastes for Asian-Western "fusion" cuisine, it's only natural that kitchen design reflects that special Eastern quality. This kitchen is a fine example of the new fusion breed that brings the philosophy of functional beauty to life. The style, while Eastern, borrows from two of the most popular Western minimalist styles: Shaker and Mission. Extensive storage, including a double cutlery drawer, two lazy Susans, and a plastic- and foil-wrap dispenser, is all hidden behind bisque-stained maple cabinetry. The small island creates balance with a rounded angle that's repeated in the high window.

Left: *Bird's-eye maple and frosted glass squares are set into the upper cabinet doors. The geometric theme is echoed in smaller squares on shelves above the black granite sink and on door hardware. Black enamel molding and black solid-surface countertops add sophisticated snap.* **Right:** *Sleek and simple, this modestly sized island possesses great flexibility. With its hard maple work surface, it fulfills many roles, from an extra chopping block to a service station for quick afternoon tea.* ***Cabinets: Plain & Fancy Custom Cabinetry.***

An Oasis of Calm

VERY CONTEMPORARY, yet as timeless as nature, this unusual kitchen is like the desert: quiet on the surface but filled with intricate surprises. The space borrows from Asian and African influences for a result that's a fresh take on modern style. A low ceiling pierced with a skylight and long, angled countertops create layers of serene horizontal planes that are at once primitive and very modern. These planes—functional countertops and display shelving—do their jobs without disrupting the restful ambience. Dramatic accent and task lighting are essential elements in themselves, modeling the room's planes and drawing attention to the handmade artwork and artifacts. The overall effect is almost curated; every element carefully selected to fulfill a visual and functional purpose.

Opposite: *Long, low shelving units in soft neutral tones, including Navajo white and honeyed wood, are cut with expanses of black granite and metal. The result? Soothing horizontal lines and ample space to showcase the owner's carefully chosen collection of artifacts and artwork.*

Inventive cabinetry creates a mini-home-office station tucked in neatly next to the fridge. A trio of small glass shelves holds books and artifacts above; below, three drawers and a storage compartment covered by a clever two-toned sliding door provide more storage.

Resource Directory

ARCHITECTS/DESIGNERS

Accent On Design
2005 De La Cruz Blvd., #145
Santa Clara, CA 95050-3035
408-988-4600
Lila Levinson, ASID, CKD, CID

Sandra E. Arabia
309 Church St. NE
Marietta, GA 30060
770-499-9015

Bauer Interior Design
3886 17th St.
San Francisco, CA 94114
415-621-7262
www.bauerdesign.com
Lou Ann Bauer

Betsey Meyer Associates
P.O. Box 1179
Water Mill, NY 11976
516-726-6428
fax 516-726-6453
Betsey Meyer, CKD, CBD

Broad Street Antiques and Collectibles
3886 Broad St., Suite C
Powder Springs, GA 30127
770-439-2029
Helen Norman

Bytner Design Associates, Inc.
20 W. Washington, Suite 6A
Clarkston, MI 48346
248-922-0065
fax 248-922-0249
bytnerdes@aol.com
www.bytnerdesign.com
Pamela Bytner, CKD

The Cabinetree Design Studio
1130 N. Nimitz Hwy., Suite A-156
Honolulu, HI 96817
808-523-9688
fax 808-523-2499
Roxanne and David Okazaki, CKDs

Canterbury Design Kitchen Interiors
103 Ridgedale Ave., P.O. Box 1115
Morristown, NJ 07960
973-539-3339
fax 973-539-2327
info@canterburydesign.com
www.canterburydesign.com
Jim Dove and Scott Seibold

Cantley and Company Inc.
2829 2nd Ave. S
Birmingham, AL 35213
205-324-2400

Lim Chang
300 N. Lake Ave., #206
Pasadena, CA 91101
626-449-9698

Charles Cunniffe Architects
610 E. Hyman Ave.
Aspen, CO 81611
970-925-5590
fax 970-925-5076
barbarak@cunniffe.com
www.cunniffe.com
Charles Cunniffe

Clodagh Design
670 Broadway, 4th floor
New York, NY 10012
212-780-5300
fax 212-780-5755
www.clodagh.com

Country Store of Seven Springs
4455 Marietta St.
Powder Springs, GA 30127
770-439-1780
fax 770-439-1708
cssevensprings@aol.com
Gloria Hilderbrand

Covenant Kitchens & Baths, Inc.
1871 Boston Post Rd.
Westbrook, CT 06498
860-399-6241
fax 860-399-8395
covenantkitchens@net.net
Gerard Ciccarello, CKD

Custom Kitchens, Inc.
6412 Horseplen Rd.
Richmond, VA 23226
804-288-7247
fax 804-282-2479
Douglas B. Leake, CKD, and Barbara Facetti

Decorating Den Interiors
19100 Montgomery Village Ave., Suite 200
Montgomery Village, MD 20886
800-DEC-DENS
www.decoratingden.com
Terri Ervin

Design for Sale, Inc.
23679 Calabasas Rd., #347
Calabasas, CA 91302
818-888-6094
fax 818-888-6095
leshay@msn.com
Andrea Leshay

Design With Maloos
550 15th St., Suite 10
San Francisco, CA 94103
415-864-3857
fax 415-864-0983
maloos@earthlink.net
www.designfinder.com/anvarian/
Maloos S. Anvarian, ASID, CCIDC

D'Image Associates
71 E. Allendale Rd.
Saddle River, NJ 07458
202-934-5420
Fran Murphy

The Downs Group
1095 Mt. Kemble Ave.
Morristown, NJ 07960
973-425-2811
Donna Martin and Jim Downs

Drury Designs, LTD
534 Pennsylvania Ave.
Glen Ellyn, IL 60137
630-469-4980
fax 630-469-2590
Gail Drury, CKD, CBD

Elements In Design
618 Island Pl.
Redwood Shores, CA 94066
650-595-8884
pennychin@elementsindesign.com
Penny Chin

Beverly Ellsley
179 Post Rd. W
Westport, CT 06880
203-227-1157

Gail Green
110 E. 59th St.
New York, NY 10022
212-909-0376

Heartwood Kitchen & Bath Design
1217 11th Ave. SW
Calgary, AB T3C 0M5 Canada
403-229-2796
fax 403-229-9790
Judy Bakalik

Honka Homes USA, Inc.
35715 U.S. Hwy. 40, Suite 303
Evergreen, CO 80439
303-679-0568
fax 303-679-0641
info@honka.com
www.honka.com

Interior Dimensions
5319 S.W. Westgate Dr., #145
Portland, OR 97221
503-292-9710
fax 503-292-0583
idteam@aol.com
Diane Gassman

Interiors by M&S
14 Clover Ln.
Roslyn Heights, NY 11577
516-484-5837
Stephanie Wolf

Jamieson Brothers Construction
RR #1, Q43
Bowen Island, BC V0N 1G0 Canada
604-947-9434

JJ Interiors
P.O. Box 5130
Chapel Hill, NC 27512
919-542-1447
Janine Jordan, CKD, IIDA, IDS

Judy King Antiques
44 Spring St.
Princeton, NJ 08540
609-279-0440
fax 609-279-0663

K. D. and Steele Cabinetry
700 E. Cherry St.
Blanchester, OH 45107
937-783-2465
fax 937-783-2466
Kimball Derrick, CKD; Jim Good; Dennis Meyer; and Joe Webb

Kitchen & Bath Design
1000 Bristol St., North #21
Newport Beach, CA 92660
949-955-1232
fax 949-955-1342
Gary White, CKD, CBD, CID

Kitchen & Bath Images
1746 General George Patton Dr.
Brentwood, TN 37027
615-377-8771
fax 615-376-9833
Vicki Edwards, CKD

Kitchen Design Studio of New Canaan, Inc.
21 South Ave.
New Canaan, CT 06840
203-966-0355
fax 203-972-5904
info@kitchendesignstudio.com
www.kitchendesignstudio.com
Greg Meyer

Kitchen Dimensions
150 S. St. Francis, C
Santa Fe, NM 87501
505-986-8820
fax 505-986-5888
Joan Viele, CKD

The Kitchen Plan Company
811 Tanglewood Dr.
Shoreview, MN 55126
651-482-0533
fax 651-482-0533
Diane L. Berndt, CKD, CBD

Kitchens & Baths By Louise Gilmartin
245-B Vine St.
Reno, NV 89503
775-332-9004
fax 775-329-9042
KBLAG@aci.net

Kitchens by Deane
1267 E. Main St.
Stamford, CT 06902
203-327-7008

Kitchens By Kieweno
4034 Broadway
Kansas City, MO 64111
816-531-3968
Randall Sisk

Kitchen Studio
5200 Eubank Blvd. NE
Albuquerque, NM 87111
505-294-6767
fax 505-294-6763
kitstu@aol.com
Joe McDermott and Diane Wandmaker, CKD

Kitchens Unique, Inc., by Lois
259 Main St., P.O. Box 689
Chester, NJ 07930
908-879-6473
fax 908-879-2446
kitunique@aol.com
Lois Perry Kirk

Kountry Kraft
P.O. Box 570
Newmanstown, PA 17073
610-589-4575
fax 800-401-0584
kountrykraft@talon.net
www.kountrykraft.com
Dee Hurst Funk, CKD

Ben Kuypers
3412 64th St. NE
Calgary, AB T1Y 4L5 Canada
403-280-8002

Le Gourmet Kitchen
2015 S. State College Blvd.
Anaheim, CA 92806
714-939-6227
fax 714-939-6334
www.legourmetkitchen.com
Bruce Colucci, CKD

Madison Design
1700 Stutz, Suite 27
Troy, MI 48084
248-643-4770

Marilyn Woods Design Associates
P.O. Box 1387
Los Altos, CA 94023-1387
650-964-9276
fax 650-964-0164
MAWoodsDES@aol.com
Marilyn Woods, CKD

Mary Kurtz Kitchens
4118 Military Rd. NW
Washington, DC 20015
mary.kurtz@ekis.com.ba
Mary Kurtz, CKD

McDonald & Moore Ltd.
82 N. 2nd St.
San Jose, CA 95113
408-292-6997
fax 408-292-5855
www.mcdonaldmoore.com

Monson Interior Design, Inc.
275 Market St., Suite 292
Minneapolis, MN 55405
612-338-0665
fax 612-338-0855
monson@mail.visi.com
Lynn Monson, ASID, CKD, CBD, CID

Murray Arnott Design Ltd.
56A Yarmouth St.
Guelph, ON N1H 4G3 Canada
519-829-1758
mail@designma.com
www.designma.com

National Kitchen & Bath Association (NKBA)
687 Willow Grove St.
Hackettstown, NJ 07840
800-843-6522

NDM Kitchens
204 E. 77th St.
New York, NY 10021
212-628-4629
Nancy Mullan

Neil Kelly Designers/ Remodelers
804 N. Alberta
Portland, OR 97217
503-288-7461
fax 503-288-7464
Karen Richmond, CKD, CBD

Olde Fields Farm
915 Sackettsford Rd.
Ivyland, PA 18974-1231
215-598-3797
Linda Daly, ASID

Barbara Ostrom
One International Blvd.
Mahwah, NJ 07495
201-529-0444

Premier Kitchens
Two Theatre Sq., Space 140
Orinda, CA 94563
925-253-9800
Victoria Reginato, CKD

Rocky Mountain Log Homes
1883 Hwy. 93 S
Hamilton, MT 59840
406-363-5680
fax 406-363-2109
sales@rmlh.com
www.rmlh.com

Rutt of Atlanta
Atlanta Decorative Arts Center, Suite 413
351 Peachtree Hills Ave. NE
Atlanta, GA 30305
404-264-9698
fax 404-265-0346
showroom@ruttatlanta.com
www.rutt.net
Pamela Goldstein Sanchez, CKD, CBD

Sieguzi Interior Designs, Inc.
218 Strathallan Wood
Toronto, ON M5N 1T4 Canada
416-785-1341
fax 416-785-9834
sieguzi.interiors@sympatico.ca
Robin Siegerman

Signature Kitchens, Inc.
2666 Charlevoix, P.O. Box 2028
Petoskey, MI 49770
616-439-0100
fax 616-439-0288

Summit Design Associates
1095 Mt. Kemble Ave.
Morristown, NJ 07960
973-425-2811
fax 973-425-2816
www.dowcon.com
Francis Giblin

Thurston Kitchen and Bath, Inc.
2920 E. 6th Ave.
Denver, CO 80206
303-399-4564
fax 303-333-4406
bonnielocke@juno.com
Greta Burandt and Deborah MacNair, CKD

Tidmore-Henry & Associates
1014 East Ave. N
Sarasota, FL 34237
941-954-4454
fax 941-955-4427
wmtidmore@aol.com
www.t-hdesigns.qpg.com

Truex, Cullins & Partners Architects
209 Battery St.
Burlington, VT 05401
802-658-2775
fax 802-658-6495
Rolf Kielman

Ultimate Kitchens
3091 S. Valley View Blvd.
Las Vegas, NV 89102
702-248-7117
fax 702-248-7119
UKLV1@LCCM.com
www.ultimatekitchens.com
Anita Brooks

JoAnne Welsh
7015 Partridge Pl.
Hyattsville, MD 20782
301-779-6181

XTC Design, Inc.
24 Forest Manor Rd.,
Suite 510
Toronto, ON M2J 1M3
Canada
416-491-3896
fax 416-491-9444
www.xtcdesign.com
Erica Westeroth

MANUFACTURERS

American Olean
1000 Cannon Ave.
Lansdale, PA 19446-1271
215-855-1111
www.americanolean.com

Bosch
2800 25th Ave.
Broadview, IL 60153
708-865-5265
www.boschappliances.com

Caldera Corp.
Pilgrim Park II
Waterbury, VT 05676
800-725-7711
fax 800-962-3072
caldera@calderacorp.com
www.calderacorp.com

Canac Kitchens
360 John St.
Thornhill, ON L3T 3M9
Canada
800-CANAC-4U

Craft-Maid Custom Kitchens, Inc.
501 S. 9th St., Bldg. C
Reading, PA 19602
610-376-8686
fax 610-376-6998

Dacor
950 S. Raymond
Pasadena, CA 91109
800-793-0093

Delta
55 E. 111th St.
Indianapolis, IN 46280
800-345-3358
www.deltafaucet.com

Downsview Kitchens
2635 Rena Rd.
Mississauga, ON L4T-1G6
Canada
905-677-9354
fax 905-677-5776
www.downsviewkitchens.com

DuPont Corian
P.O. Box 80012
Wilmington, DE 19880-0702
800-4-CORIAN
www.corian.com

Dynasty Range
7355 Slauson Ave.
Commerce, CA 90040
323-889-4888
www.dynastyrange.com

Elkay
222 Camden Ct.
Oak Brook, IL 60523
630-574-8484
fax 630-574-5012
www.elkay.com

Fireclay Tile
495 W. Julian
San Jose, CA 95110
408-275-1182
www.fireclaytile.com

FSC Wallcoverings, a division of F. Schumacher & Co.
79 Madison Ave.
New York, NY 10016
www.fsco.com

GE Appliances
Appliance Park
Bldg. 3, Rm. 232
Louisville, KY 40225
800-626-2000
www.appliances.com

Grohe America, Inc.
241 Covington Dr.
Bloomingdale, IL 60108
708-582-7711

Heritage Custom Kitchens
215 Diller Ave.
New Holland, PA 17557
717-354-4011
www.hck.com

Horton Brasses
Nooks Hill Rd., P.O. Box 95
Cromwell, CT 06416
860-635-4400
www.horton-brasses.com

KitchenAid
2023 Pipestone Rd.
Benton Harbor, MI 49022
800-422-1230
www.kitchenaid.com

Kohler Company
444 Highland Dr.
Kohler, WI 53044
800-4-KOHLER
www.kohlerco.com

LBL Lighting
320 W. 202nd St.
Chicago, IL 60411
800-323-3226

Lightolier
631 Airport Rd.
Fall River, MA 02720
508-769-8131
fax 508-674-4710
www.lightolier.com

Mark Wilkinson Furniture, Ltd.
Overton House, High Street
Bromham, Chippenham
Wiltshire SN15 2HA England
011-44-1380-850004
fax 011-44-1380-850184

Merit Kitchens
1-6130 4th St. SE
Calgary, AB T2H 2B6 Canada
403-252-0334
fax 403-255-0646

Miele
Nine Independence Way
Princeton, NJ 08540
800-843-7231
www.mieleusa.com

Neff Kitchens
Six Melanie Dr.
Brampton, ON L6T 4K9
Canada
905-791-7770
fax 905-791-7788

Neidhardt Lighting
1760 Cesar Chavez St., Unit C
San Francisco, CA 94124
800-978-8828

Plain & Fancy Custom Cabinetry
Oak Street & Rt. 501,
P.O. Box 519
Schaefferstown, PA 17088
717-949-6571
fax 717-949-2114

Premier Custom Built Cabinets
110 Short St.
New Holland, PA 17557
717-354-3059

Rutt Custom Cabinetry
P.O. Box 129
Goodville, PA 17528
215-445-6751
www.rutt1.com

Seabrook Wallcoverings, Inc.
1325 Farmville Rd.
Memphis, TN 38122
800-238-9152
fax 901-320-3673
www.seabrookwallcoverings.com

SieMatic Corporation
Two Greenwood Sq.
3331 Street Rd., Suite 450
Bensalem, PA 19020
215-244-6800
fax 215-244-6822

Snaidero USA
8687 Melrose Ave., Suite G236
Los Angeles, CA 90069
310-657-3224
fax 310-657-1149
www.snaidero-usa.com

Sub-Zero Freezer Co., Inc.
4717 Hammersley Rd.
Madison, WI 53711
800-222-7820
www.subzero.com

Sub-Zero Freezer Co., Inc.
Clarke Distributors
63 South St.
Hopkinton, MA 01748
508-435-6226
fax 508-435-6860
www.clarkecorp.com

Subtle
71 Queens Rd.
Buckhurst Hill, Essex 1G9 5BW England
011-10-1815-053272
fax 011-10-1815-053770

T.L. Precision Cabinets
Bay G, 7210 5th St. SE
Calgary, AB T2H 2L9 Canada
403-273-2246

Thermador
5551 McFadden Ave.
Huntington Beach, CA 92649
800-656-9226
www.thermador.com

Ultra Craft
6163 Old 421 Rd.
Liberty, NC 27298
336-622-4281
www.ultracraft.com

Valcucine USA
152 Wooster St.
New York, NY 10012
212-253-5969
fax 212-253-5889
www.valcucine.it

Vent-A-Hood
51 Corsica Dr.
Newport Beach, CA 92660
972-235-2501
www.ventahood.com

Viking
111 Front St.
Greenwood, MS 38930
888-845-4641
www.vikingrange.com

Wilsonart
2400 Wilson Pl.,
P.O. Box 6110
Temple, TX 76503-6110
800-433-3222
fax 254-207-2384
www.wilsonart.com

Wolf Range
19600 S. Alameda St.
Compton, CA 90221
800-366-9653

Wood-Mode
One 2nd St.
Kreamer, PA 17833
800-635-7500
www.wood-mode.com

York Wallcoverings
750 Linden Ave.
York, PA 17405
800-375-YORK
AD@yorkwall.com
212-532-9105

PHOTOGRAPHERS

Abode Interiors UK
Albion Court
Cheshire, SK11 6ER England
011-44-1625-500070
fax 011-44-1625-500910

Arcaid
The Factory, Two Acre Rd.
Kingston on Thames
Surrey KT2 6EP England
011-44-1815-464352
fax 011-44-1815-415230

Dean J. Birinyi
P.O. Box 545
Englewood, CO 80151
303-762-0583

Blue Door Studios
2011 Bowness Rd. NW
Calgary, AB T2N 3K9 Canada
403-217-2362
bluedoorstudios@cadvision.com
Barb Kelsall

Craig Burleigh
2112 Lyon Ave.
Belmont, CA 94002
650-551-1155

Carolyn L. Bates Photography
20 Caroline St.
Burlington, VT 05401
802-862-5386
fax 802-862-5286
batesphoto@aol.com

Dave Carter
1001 W. Steven Ave., #416
Santa Ana, CA 92707
714-557-8754

Christopher Dew Productions
95 Gloucester St.
Toronto, ON M4Y 1M2 Canada
416-964-6107
fax 416-967-0863

Philip Clayton-Thompson
7866 S.E. 16th Ave.
Portland, OR 97202
503-234-4883
fax 503-234-5693

Stephen Cridland
1231 N.W. Hoyt St., Suite 306
Portland, OR 97209
503-274-0954

Daniel Aubrey Photography
100 W. 23rd St., 5th floor
New York, NY 10011
212-414-0014
fax 212-414-0013
danaubry@aol.com

Elizabeth Whiting & Associates
21 Albert St.
London NW1 7LU England
011-44-1713-882828
fax 011-44-1713-871615
Brian Harrison

Exposures Unlimited
4390 Wallace Rd.
Oxford, OH 45056
513-523-2579
Ron Kolb

Tony Giammarino
419 Williamsdale Dr.
Richmond, VA 23235-4059
804-320-9709
fax 804-320-3012
giamfoto@home.com

David Glomb
458½ N. Genesee Ave.
Los Angeles, CA 90036
323-655-4491
fax 323-651-1437

Bob Greenspan
3700 E. Broadway
Kansas City, MO 64111
816-931-2555

Nancy Hill
210 Mamanasco Rd.
Ridgefield, CT 06877
203-431-7655
fax 203-431-7655

The Interior Archive, Ltd.
401 Fulham Rd.
London SW6 1EB England
011-44-1713-700595
fax 011-44-1819-602695

Jeffrey Green Photography
4440 Marengo Pl.
Las Vegas, NV 89147
800-257-4347

Kaskel Architectural Photography
P.O. Box 2511
Glenview, IL 60025
773-960-9091
Mike Kaskel

Kitchen & Bath Images
1746 General George Patton Dr.
Brentwood, TN 37027
615-377-8771
fax 615-376-9833
Bill LaFevor

Peter Ledwith
622 E. 20th St.
New York, NY 10009
212-460-8404
fax 212-228-1398

Vincent Lisanti
330 Clinton Ave.
Dobbs Ferry, NY 10522
914-693-5273

David Duncan Livingston
1036 Erica Rd.
Mill Valley, CA 94941
415-383-0898

Dan Mayers
416 W. 23rd St., #2C
New York, NY 10011
212-989-1871
fax 212-989-1871

Melabee Miller Photography
29 Beechwood Pl.
Hillside, NJ 07205
908-527-9121

Rob Melnychuk
1587 W. 8th Ave., Suite 401
Vancouver, BC V6J 1T5 Canada
604-736-8066

Karen Melvin
605 7th St. SE
Minneapolis, MN 55414
612-379-7925

Bradley Olman
145 Oakland St.
Red Bank, NJ 07701
732-450-2050
fax 732-345-8212
olmanphoto@aol.com

Phillip Ennis Photography
114 Millertown Rd.
Bedford, NY 10506
914-234-9574
fax 914-234-0360
phillipe@cloud9.net

Quadra Focus Photography
588 Waite Ave.
Sunnyvale, CA 94086
408-739-1465
fax 408-739-9117
John Canham

Raef Grohne Architectural Photographer
Suite 1103-1323 Homer St.
Vancouver, BC V6B 5T1 Canada
604-688-9407
raef@raefgrohne.com
www.raefgrohne.com

Randall McKinney Photography
115 Sunnyside Ave.
Mill Valley, CA 94941
415-389-6408

Real Images Architectural Photography
3003 Mulberry St.
Marietta, GA 30066
678-290-7800
fax 678-290-7722
John Umberger

Samu Studio
10 Nelson Ave.
Blue Point, NY 11715
212-754-0415

Brad Simmons
3591 Cocanougher Rd., P.O. Box 97
Perryville, KY 40468
606-332-8400
fax 606-332-4433

Beth Singer
25741 River Dr.
Franklin, MI 48025
248-626-4860
fax 248-932-3496

Tim Street-Porter Photography
2074 Watsonia Terrace
Los Angeles, CA 90068
323-874-4278

Photo Credits

Front cover: **Brian Harrison, Elizabeth Whiting & Associates**
Back cover: **Tim Street-Porter Photography**
Abode Interiors UK: 61, 182, 183, 270, 271; **Accent On Design/Quadra Focus Photography, John Canham:** 28, 130, 131, 178, 179, 222, 225; **Arcaid:** Richard Bryant: 181 (bottom), 192; Nicholas Kane: 99 (bottom), 104; Alan Weintraub: 106, 107, 305 (top), 312, 313; **Betsey Meyer Associates/Peter Ledwith:** 152, 153, 226, 227; **Bytner Design Associates, Inc./John Murphy:** 46; **The Cabinetree Design Studio/Macario:** 11 (top), 16, 30; **Canac Kitchens:** 196, 197, 220 (bottom), 225; **Canterbury Design Kitchen Interiors:** 200 (top), 202, 203; Steven Tex: 40, 238, 239, 253 (bottom); **Cantley and Company Inc./Harris Pander Studio:** 135 (top), 142, 143, 156, 157; **Carolyn L. Bates Photography/Downsview Kitchens:** 41 (top), 181 (top), 190; **Charles Cunniffe Architects:** Dean J. Birinyi: 186, 187; Steve Mundinger: 54 (top), 140, 141; Steve Mundinger/Dave Marlow: 60; **Philip Clayton-Thompson:** 50 (top right), 84, 85, 96, 97; **Covenant Kitchens & Baths, Inc./Jim Fiora Studio:** 36 (bottom); **Daniel Aubrey Photography:** 304 (bottom), 306, 307; **Decorating Den Interiors/Bradley Olman:** 174, 175; **Design for Sale, Inc./David Glomb:** 218, 219; **Design With Maloos/Randall McKinney Photography:** 8; **The Downs Group/James Prince:** 286, 287; **Downsview Kitchens/Michael Mahovlich:** 181 (top), 190; **Elaine Siegel Associates/Wood-Mode:** 6, 37, 146, 147, 148, 232 (center), 244, 245, 285 (center), 302, 303; **Elements In Design/Mert Carpenter:** 176, 177; **Elkay:** 44 (bottom); **FSC Wallcoverings:** 51 (top left); **Tony Giammarino:** 45, 78, 79; **Bob Greenspan:** 159 (bottom), 170, 171, 298, 299; **Heartwood Kitchen & Bath Design/G. Killiam Lane/Masterworks:** 35 (top); **Nancy Hill:** 42, 57, 74, 75, 111 (bottom), 122, 123, 158 (top), 160, 161, 200 (bottom), 204, 205; **Honka Homes USA, Inc.**: 275 (bottom); **The Interior Archive, Ltd.**: Simon McBride: 201 (bottom), 212, 213; Fritz von der Schulenburg: 41 (bottom), 233 (center), 242, 243, 252; **Interior Dimensions/Stephen Cridland:** 220 (top), 223; **JJ Interiors/Vincent Lisanti:** 34, 118, 119; **Kaskel Architectural Photography, Mike Kaskel:** 9 (bottom), 246, 247; **K. D. and Steele Cabinetry:** 214, 215, 233 (bottom), 240, 241; Exposures Unlimited, Ron Kolb: 284 (bottom), 294, 295; Kaskel Architectural Photography, Mike Kaskel: 50 (bottom left); **Kitchen & Bath Design, Gary White/Larry A. Falke:** 54 (bottom), 56, 124, 125, 172, 173; **Kitchen Design Studio of New Canaan, Inc./David Sloane Photography:** 21; **Kitchen Dimensions/Knight Photography:** 50 (top left), 53; **Kitchens & Baths By Louise Gilmartin/Leonard Lammi:** 27, 120, 121, 135 (bottom), 138, 139, 144, 145; **Kitchen Studio/Jerry Rabinowitz:** 25 (bottom); **Kitchens Unique, Inc., by Lois:** Peter Leach: 284 (top), 285 (bottom), 290, 291, 292, 293; Dan Murro: 14, 32; **Kountry Kraft:** 300, 301; **Le Gourmet Kitchen/Dave Carter:** 17, 111 (top), 116; **David Duncan Livingston:** 29, 35 (bottom), 59, 67 (top & center), 110 (bottom), 114, 115, 184, 185, 224, 253 (top); **Log Home Living/Murray Arnott Design Ltd./Raef Grohne Architectural Photographer:** 276, 277; **Marilyn Woods Design Associates/Craig Burleigh:** 11 (bottom); **Mark Wilkinson Furniture, Ltd.:** 49 (bottom), 67 (bottom); **Mary Kurtz Kitchens/Vickie Lewis:** 12; **Dan Mayers:** courtesy of *Country Collectibles* magazine: Contents (right center), 82, 83, 260, 261, 264; courtesy of *Country Kitchens* magazine: 71, 72, 73, 80, 86, 87, 88, 89, 90, 91, 158 (bottom), 166, 167, 254 (top); **McDonald & Moore Ltd.:** 232 (top), 250, 251; **Melabee Miller Photography:** 25 (top), 134 (bottom), 149; **Rob Melnychuk:** Contents (left center), 55, 136, 137, 267 (bottom), 282, 283; **Merit Kitchens/Ben Kuypers/Blue Door Studios, Barb Kelsall:** 132, 133; **Monson Interior Design, Inc./Karen Melvin:** 9 (top); **National Kitchen & Bath Association:** Joan Des Combes/Christopher Hornsby: 50 (bottom right); Drury Designs, LTD/David Duncan Livingston: 164, 165; Kitchen & Bath Images/Bill LaFevor: 216, 217; Kitchens Unique, Inc., by Lois/Anthony Isreal: 31; Neil Kelly Designers/Remodelers/David Duncan Livingston: 168, 169; **Bradley Olman:** courtesy of *Country Collectibles* magazine: 51 (top right), 81, 134 (top), 150, 151; **Phillip Ennis Photography:** Lim Chang: 112, 113; D'Image Associates, Fran Murphy: 201 (center), 206 ; Beverly Ellsley: 305 (bottom), 308, 309; Gail Green: 98 (top), 102, 103; Interiors by M&S, Stephanie Wolf: 43 (bottom); NDM Kitchens, Nancy Mullan: 26; Barbara Ostrom: Contents (bottom left), 63 (top), 65 (bottom), 201 (top), 207, 208, 209, 232 (bottom), 234, 235; **Plain & Fancy Custom Cabinetry:** 304 (top), 310, 311; **Premier Kitchens, Victoria Reginato/Kathleen Bellesiles:** 10; **Real Images Architectural Photography, John Umberger:** 65 (top), 221 (top), 228, 229; **Samu Studio, Ken Kelly:** Contents (bottom right), 64, 256, 257; **Seabrook Wallcoverings, Inc.**: 36 (top), 62; **Sieguzi Interior Designs, Inc./Big Red Photography, John Scully:** 180 (bottom), 188, 189; **Brad Simmons:** 66, 70, 92, 93, 94, 95, 255 (top), 262, 263, 268, 269; **Beth Singer:** 4, 76, 77, 99 (top), 108, 109, 154, 155, 198, 199, 210, 211, 221 (bottom), 230, 231, 248, 249, 285 (top), 288, 289, 296, 297; **Snaidero USA:** 193; **Spiker Communications, Inc./Rocky Mountain Log Homes:** 266, 267 (top & center), 272, 273, 274, 275 (top), 278, 279, 280, 281; **Subtle/Dave Dacby:** 105; **Sub-Zero Freezer Co. Inc., Clarke Distributors:** 44 (top); **Thurston Kitchen and Bath, Inc./Susan English Photography:** 58; **Tim Street-Porter Photography:** Contents (top), 7, 18, 23, 24, 33, 38, 49 (top), 68, 98 (bottom), 100, 101, 254 (bottom), 255 (bottom), 258, 259; **T.L. Precision Cabinets/Ben Kuypers/Blue Door Studios, Barb Kelsall:** 110 (top); 126, 127, 128, 129; **Ultimate Kitchens:** Anita Brooks/Jeffrey Green Photography: 233 (top), 236, 237; Colours, Inc./Jeffrey Green Photography: 117; **Valcucine USA:** G. Centazzo: 43 (top), 48, 51 (bottom); Studio ikon: 180 (top), 191; **Village:** 63 (bottom); **Jessie Walker:** 159 (top), 162, 163, 265; **Wilsonart/Robert Germany:** 52; **XTC Design, Inc./Christopher Dew Productions:** 181 (center), 194, 195; **York Wallcoverings:** 13, 15, 20.